BRITAIN
IN CONTEXT

BRITAIN IN CONTEXT

JOHN D. HEY

assisted by Desmond Delahunt, John Dorland,
Patrick Figgis, Ian Jewitt, Heather Lindstrom,
Anne Ludbrook, Ashley Shirlin, Len Smith and
Jayne Wilde

ST. MARTIN'S · NEW YORK

To my brother,
David Hey

For information write:
St. Martin's Press, Inc., 175 Fifth Ave., New York, NY 10010

ISBN: 0-312-09741-7
Library of Congress Catalog Card Number: 79-66554
First published in the U.K. and the U.S.A. in 1979

21 Jan '80

Phototypeset in VIP Times by
Western Printing Services Ltd, Bristol
Printed in Great Britain by
Ebenezer Baylis and Son Ltd, Leicester
and bound at
Kemp Hall Bindery, Oxford

CONTENTS

(* denotes international comparisons)

The Public Authorities

Industry

Labour

Finance

BRITAIN AS A SOCIETY OF INDIVIDUALS

The Vital Statistics of Britain

Income, Taxation and Spending

Other Aspects of Society

ACKNOWLEDGEMENTS

The original idea, and the motivating force, behind this book comes from Richard Blackwell. All credit is therefore due to him for all that is praiseworthy about the book; any deficiencies are almost certainly the result of the suggestions of his that I ignored.

All the hard work involved in the writing of this book was performed by my team of assistants: Desmond Delahunt, John Dorland, Patrick Figgis, Ian Jewitt, Heather Lindstrom, Anne Ludbrook, Ashley Shirlin, Len Smith and Jayne Wilde. To them, hearty thanks for their toil and artistic fervour.

The aesthetic achievement of turning the team's hard work into an elegant and attractive book was begun most nobly by Mrs. Jo Hall and Miss Jackie Farnell who produced an impeccable typescript unbelievably quickly. David Martin proffered encouragement and help throughout.

The book as a whole was helped along its path to fruition by my wife's constant encouragement.

INTRODUCTION

The purpose of this book, as its title indicates, is to portray Britain in *context*. It is designed to present Britain both in a temporal context and in a world context; to place the Britain of today in perspective, relative both to the rest of the world, and to the Britain of yesterday.

Moreover, this book is intended to portray Britain *as it is*; not as optimists would wish it were, nor as pessimists would have us believe it is, but rather as it actually is. It has no particular axe to grind, no special message to deliver, other than to present a true portrayal of Britain—dimples, freckles, warts, and all.

It is hoped that the book will provide an unbiased, unprejudiced picture of Britain that can be used as an impartial source of reference, an arbiter in policy discussions on Britain's past, present and future role in the world and status as an individual country. Moreover, it is specifically designed so that the information is presented pictorially in a manner as attractive, appealing and easily accessible as possible, as the reader will immediately see on turning over the pages. It is in this respect, therefore, that this book differs from other sources of impartial information about Britain; all too often, they present such information in an unappealing format (almost invariably in the form of statistical tables) that makes them largely indigestible except to the expert. It is not at the expert that *Britain in Context* is aimed; rather it is at the intelligent layman who wishes to gain an objective view of Britain *as it is*. Ultimately, this book's purpose is to dispel the half-remembered truths, badly digested statistics and deliberately distorted statements, and replace them by a fair portrayal of Britain *in context*.

Clearly, any attempt to portray *all* the economic information of relevance to Britain (or which might conceivably be found of interest by someone) would be doomed to failure: the resulting volume (or, rather, volumes!) would simply be enormous. The initial task in designing this book, therefore, was to exercise judgement in selecting those aspects of Britain which were likely to be of most interest and of greatest importance in obtaining a fair description of Britain in context. To this end, three broad categories were adopted—these correspond to the three main parts of the book. The first part examines *Britain as Part of the World*, and concentrates on those particular aspects that are of interest when discussing Britain's role in the world and when comparing Britain with other countries. The second part describes *Britain as an Economic Aggregate*, and focuses attention on the main aspects of Britain as an economic unit. Finally, the third part explores *Britain as a Society of Individuals*, and describes the situation of the individual (person or household) in Britain today and how it compares with other countries and other times.

Within each of these three main parts, the same kinds of criteria have

1

been applied to the selection of topics for discussion: What information is needed to portray in an unbiased fashion the most important features of Britain in the specific context under discussion? What information would be of interest to the reader—in particular, what aspects of these topics are currently being hotly debated by the interested and intelligent layman? Occasionally, these criteria led to conflicting choices; but this was relatively rare—in general, the topics being publicly debated usually coincide with the most important aspects of the issue in hand.

Throughout the book, the material is organized by topic, eighty-seven in all. Each topic is presented on two facing pages. The left-hand pages are devoted to verbal accounts of each topic and of the pictorial representation of the information on each right-hand page. Cross-references are sometimes given to related topics.

On the right-hand pages I have tried to present the material in as attractive a manner as possible, using a variety of devices—including bar charts, pie charts, occasional tables and time-series graphs. Most of these methods will be familiar to the reader, and any unusual presentation is explained and discussed on the related left-hand page.

The material on each left-hand page is divided generally into three sections. The first, and usually the most important, discusses the main points and summarizes the information displayed on the right. Where possible, answers to the question 'Why is the situation as it is ?' are given. However, such explanations are omitted where personal bias or politics may creep in; the book is intended to remain on solid objective ground. The second section contains a description of the data that have been used, and a commentary on any manipulations necessary. Where there are grounds for doubting the validity, or accuracy, or relevance, of the data, comment will be made. (Some more will be said on this point later in this introduction.) The third, and final, section on the left-hand page is a statement of the major data sources, so that the interested reader can pursue particular topics of interest further. Complete bibliographical details will be found towards the end of the book, just before the index.

The first part, *Britain as Part of the World*, contains sixteen topics. These sixteen topics are chosen on the basis of one or other (or both) of two criteria: first, to compare certain key features of Britain (both now and in the past) with the same key features of other important countries in the world (both now and in the past); secondly, to examine the relationship between Britain and the rest of the world, particularly with respect to its trading position. The first five topics are good examples of topics included under the former category; topic 1 examines Britain's position in the 'income per head' league table among EEC countries; topic 2 carries out a similar analysis though using a broader international comparison; topic 3 compares international economic growth rates, while topic 4 looks at industrial output; topic 5 examines the vexed question of inflation, and explores how Britain's inflation rate has moved relative to that of other countries. The last six topics in this part show Britain's relationship with the rest of the world, as revealed through its trading position. For example, topics 11 and 12 show how Britain's share of world trade has changed through time, while topics 14 and 15 show how the components (both on a geographical and on a goods breakdown) of Britain's trade have moved.

The second part, *Britain as an Economic Aggregate*, is the largest part, containing thirty-nine topics. It is sub-divided into five parts; the first looks at the economy as a whole, while the remaining four each examine some major component of the total. A brief description of these follows. The first, containing eight topics, looks at the economy as a whole as measured using the aggregate economic concepts of *National Income, Expenditure and Output*. This section, thus, naturally revolves around Gross Domestic Product (GDP) as an indicator of economic welfare; the first topic looks at GDP in general, while the remaining seven topics all examine different aspects of the composition of GDP. Included within these topics are descriptions of the behaviour of two of the more important components of GDP, namely, consumers' expenditure and capital formation. The second, with ten topics, explores the role and effect of *The Public Authorities* within Britain. A comparison with other countries' experience is an important feature of this section. Amongst the topics discussed in this section are the degree of public authority involvement with education, health and defence, and an examination of different countries' relative dependence on different methods of revenue-raising. The third, with eight topics, examines the state of *Industry* in Britain; it contains some relevant international comparisons. Amongst the topics discussed in this section are hours of work, the crucial questions of investment and energy consumption, and the relative profitability of the private and public sectors in Britain. The ten topics in the fourth scrutinize the role and importance of the *Labour* market in Britain. Of particular interest in this section is the description of unemployment both internationally and within Britain; the British case is analysed by its regional and durational components. The other main themes in this section are the strength and composition of the trade union movement, and the relative magnitude of industrial stoppages (in both temporal and geographical perspective). The final section, containing just three topics, briefly examines the world of *Finance*.

The third part, *Britain as a Society of Individuals*, contains thirty-two topics, and is divided up into three sections. The first of these three sections describes the *Vital Statistics of Britain*, and, in many instances, compares them with similarly vital statistics for other countries. Naturally, the main features discussed in this section concern the vital stages of life: birth, marriage, divorce, migration, suicide, and death. The inter-action of all of these, of course, leads to the actual population distribution which is the concern of the first topic. In addition, the changing length of life expectancy, and the incidence of infectious diseases are discussed. The second section's eleven topics explore *Income, Taxation and Spending*, particularly as these affect the individual person or household. The first two topics briefly examine two distributional problems which are currently the issue of much debate: the distribution of wealth and the distribution of income. Elsewhere in this section are topics on the rate of inflation (both of prices and of incomes) and on the consequent changes in real incomes. The changing nature of taxation is discussed, as well as the changing composition of household spending patterns. The final section containing nine topics, looks at *Other Aspects of Society* that have not been treated elsewhere. Of necessity, this is a rather wide-ranging section, consisting of topics that do not fit neatly into the categorization scheme employed throughout the remainder of the book. The section begins by looking at crime; three topics are then devoted to an international comparison of different modes of passenger transport: specifically, car, air, and rail. Also included in this section are topics on road accidents and on tourism, while the concluding three topics discuss different aspects of what might loosely be regarded as cultural aspects of society: namely, newspapers, cinemas and education.

Although the categorization scheme adopted is sufficiently wide to include most aspects of Britain that might be considered relevant or interesting, the fact that the total number of topics is restricted to eighty-seven inevitably means that some aspects have had to be omitted or left insufficiently explored. However, an attempt has been made to 'satisfy most people most of the time', and I hope that this objective has been met.

Apart from topics that did not appear sufficiently important to merit inclusion, some that are manifestly important have been deliberately omitted, usually because of the poor quality of the available data. Rather than include rather dubious material, it seemed preferable to omit the topic altogether.

Occasionally, some topics overlap. In such cases, it appeared preferable to suffer some duplication rather than to present lop-sided data, the importance of which could be appreciated only by referring to other topics. But as far as possible, the topics should be able to stand alone.

The reader is urged to use the index in addition to the contents page in order to find the relevant information. In many cases, the index is considerably more informative than the contents page; indeed, in some cases the topic title (in the interests of brevity) may not be clear to the average reader. Thus, what appears to be an omission from the contents page may turn out not to be so in the index.

A few final points must be made. First, throughout this introduction and in the title of the book, 'Britain' is used to mean 'the United Kingdom'. I hope that readers will allow this small amount of poetic licence in an otherwise factual account (and that readers in Northern Ireland will not be offended).

More importantly, and substantively, is the question of data. Throughout this introduction, and indeed throughout the rest of the book, the intention to present an unbiased, impartial, view of Britain has been stressed. To this end, a continuing attempt has been made to select the information used in each topic in as an unbiased fashion as possible. In many cases, this objective is fairly easily achieved; in others, it is more difficult; while there are cases where 'objective evidence' seems almost a contradiction in terms. As has already been noted, these latter cases have been deliberately omitted. However, there are innumerable cases where the data is 'quite' objective; these have been included (indeed, if all ever-so-slightly dubious cases were omitted from this book, it would be very thin). Also included are some topics almost on the borderline for omission (an obvious case in this category is topic 68 on the distribution of wealth). In all such topics, where there is some ambiguity over the 'objectivity' of the data, discussion is included in the 'data' section of the topic. Such qualifications are crucial in drawing conclusions from the information.

This kind of problem frequently occurs when international comparisons are carried out. Since different countries simply have different legal, institutional and social frameworks, it is often meaningless to try to measure a particular concept in the same way for all. This problem is often compounded by the differing methods by which statistical information is collected in different countries. The resulting statistics are, quite often, simply 'incomparable'. As far as is possible, this book uses data that helps to reconcile international differences in defining statistical concepts and collecting information. (The magnitude of these differences can be seen in topic 43, which presents both 'unreconciled' and 'reconciled' data on the same economic variables.) Any residual problems of comparability are discussed in the 'data' sections of the topics; again such comments should be used to qualify any inferences drawn.

For the international comparisons I have tried to select a reasonably wide range of countries and to avoid bias. Occasionally, problems of data availability overrode the first of these two criteria. Consistency (over the different sections) was also clearly an important criterion. The actual number of countries to be included in the international comparisons was largely determined by aesthetic considerations; in many cases, attempting to portray more than a total of six countries would simply have led to visual confusion.

Finally, the time period covered. The starting date was chosen by informational considerations or by data availability, whichever led to the earliest starting data. (All too often, the lack of data constrained topic coverage—particularly those involving international comparisons.) The

5

finishing date was chosen by data availability. As will be obvious, data relating to Britain alone is much more up-to-date than that employed in international comparisons. Generally, the most recently published data was used wherever possible. (This just goes to show how efficient Britain's Central Statistical Office is relative to some of its overseas counterparts!) other qualifications appear in the relevant places.

Next are the topics themselves; in these, it is hoped, will be found Britain *in context*.

Britain as Part of the World

1 INCOME PER HEAD IN THE EEC

In comparing the relative standards of living of members of the European Economic Community (EEC), figures of Gross Domestic Product (GDP), which is considered to be an appropriate measure of a country's total production of goods and services, are divided by the corresponding population figures to give *per capita* gross domestic product data. There are many problems, however, in comparing these results. The most important of these concern the use of exchange rates to convert all currencies into one, which, as in this case, is usually American dollars ($). These exchange rates are subject to considerable fluctuation and cannot, therefore, accurately convert one currency to another when averaged out over a year. Other problems include the fact that quality of goods and services produced is not taken into consideration, that price levels are different in each country, and that no consideration is made of income distribution.

Although the EEC did not exist in 1953 as we know it today—Britain, for example, did not join until 1973—the diagrams opposite show the comparative living standards of the nine current member countries. They show that since 1953 the United Kingdom has slipped from fourth to seventh place, being overtaken by Denmark, West Germany and the Netherlands. West Germany has continued to recover from the Second World War, although even this recovery is not sufficient to overtake the 1975 'winner', Denmark, which profits from its relatively small size. Most of the other countries have maintained an average and steady improvement in living standards, although Italy has now handed over the 'wooden spoon' to Ireland, who, along with Britain and Denmark, joined the EEC in the early 1970s.

Source

United Nations Yearbook of National Accounts Statistics

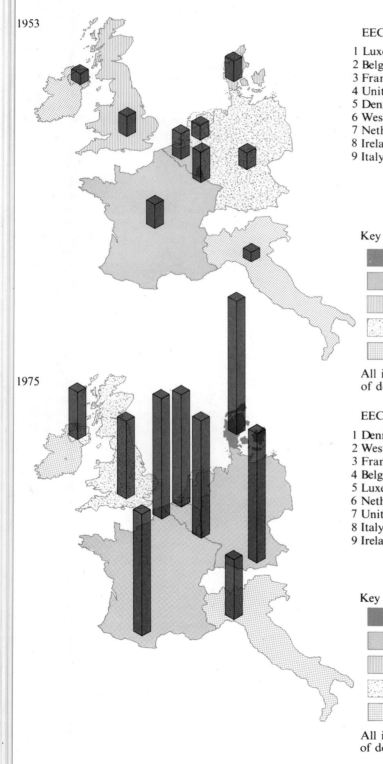

1953

Key

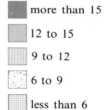

more than 15

12 to 15

9 to 12

6 to 9

less than 6

All in hundreds
of dollars per head

1975

Key

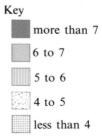

more than 7

6 to 7

5 to 6

4 to 5

less than 4

All in thousands
of dollars per head

2 GROSS DOMESTIC PRODUCT PER HEAD

In 1953 the United States and Canada had the highest *per capita* Gross Domestic Product, with Britain in ninth place. Britain had not been so badly damaged in the Second World War as had some other countries, notably West Germany, so these figures must be seen in the light of the fact that these countries were having to rebuild their industries. By 1965 Germany, Japan and Italy were catching up Britain and were also gaining ground on the United States. But even so, Britain was still substantially ahead of them, having a *per capita* GDP of nearly double that of Japan.

The next ten years, however, changed all that. West Germany shot ahead of Britain to reach seventh place in the 'top ten' countries, coming close to the United States, who had lost first position to Switzerland. Japan too more than doubled its GDP per head of population, overtaking Britain but as yet not challenging the top ten. Italy also improved its position relative to Britain's, although not relative to the rest of the world. Britain's fall to nineteenth place came as more European countries overtook her, along with Saudi Arabia, who gained eighteenth place in 1975.

Data

Comparisons of GDP per head of population are made difficult by the problems that were discussed in topic 1. They also give only one way of comparing living standards, ignoring factors of 'quality of life' such as beautiful countryside that might benefit the inhabitants of one country more than those of another. To include the effect of such factors though would be difficult.

All the figures shown are again in 1975 prices.

Source

United Nations Yearbook of National Accounts Statistics
International Labour Office, Yearbook of Labour Statistics

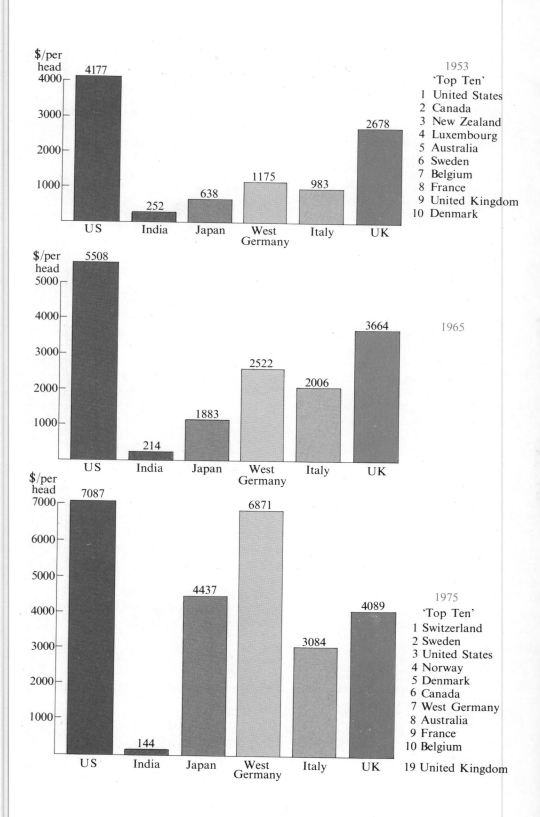

3 RATES OF GROWTH OF GDP

The rates of growth of GDP are shown opposite for three time periods. For the ten years between 1950 and 1960 Britain had the lowest rate of growth (2.7 per cent), while Germany and Japan, whose economies were still recovering from the war years, were growing at average rates of 7.9 per cent and 7.7 per cent respectively.

Britain, however, continued to have a slow rate of growth, again falling short between 1960 and 1970 of India. Germany's rate of growth had by this time fallen to a more modest 4.6 per cent, which still compared well with the growth rates of the United States, 4.3 per cent, and Italy, 5.3 per cent, although Japan, in the middle of an economic boom, had an average annual growth rate of 10.5 per cent. This huge growth rate decreased over the third period of 1970–75 to 6.8 per cent, with all countries' rates falling together as a result of the adverse economic conditions that existed at the start of the 1970s. Britain's growth rate of 2.3 per cent is now comparable to those of other major industrial nations (US, 2.5 per cent and West Germany, 2.2 per cent) but this slower growth has meant falling living standards and higher unemployment.

Capital per worker employed, although of dubious accuracy, shows the relative amount of capital, which includes buildings and machinery, each country has for its labour force. Again Britain fares badly, coming in last among the five countries shown. India has been omitted because no data are available.

Data

Rates of growth establish how much each country's GDP has changed over the year relative to the previous year. When these rates are averaged out over a five or ten year period, to smooth freak results, the diagrams as shown are obtained. For the last time period, however, figures for India, Japan and Italy are only quoted for the period 1970–74.

The capital per worker employed is subject to several limitations. Gross fixed capital formation is in the country's individual currency, so conversions to a common denominator of American dollars are one cause of inaccuracy. The second concerns the fluctuating nature of the labour force and differing methods of measuring labour forces. The results shown here, therefore, should be viewed in the light of these misgivings.

Sources

Statistical Yearbook
International Labour Office, Yearbook of Labour Statistics
Yearbook of National Accounts Statistics

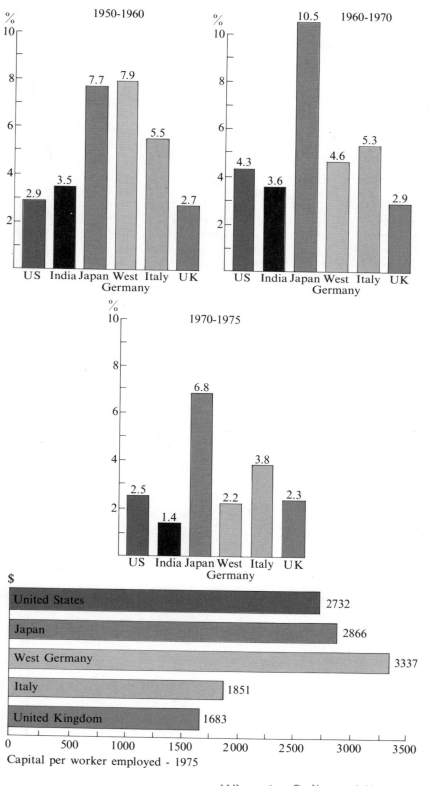

1950-1960

%
10 —
8 —
6 —
4 —
2 —

| US | India | Japan | West Germany | Italy | UK |
| 2.9 | 3.5 | 7.7 | 7.9 | 5.5 | 2.7 |

1960-1970

%
10.5
10 —
8 —
6 —
4 —
2 —

| US | India | Japan | West Germany | Italy | UK |
| 4.3 | 3.6 | 10.5 | 4.6 | 5.3 | 2.9 |

1970-1975

%
10 —
8 —
6 —
4 —
2 —

| US | India | Japan | West Germany | Italy | UK |
| 2.5 | 1.4 | 6.8 | 2.2 | 3.8 | 2.3 |

$

United States — 2732
Japan — 2866
West Germany — 3337
Italy — 1851
United Kingdom — 1683

0   500   1000   1500   2000   2500   3000   3500

Capital per worker employed - 1975

4 INDUSTRIAL PRODUCTION

Japan's economic emergence since 1958 is shown to good effect by the diagram opposite. It shows that in 1973 Japan reached a peak of production that was nearly seven times the corresponding level in 1958, increasing its share of total world production as a result from 3.3 per cent in 1958 to 10.4 per cent in 1974. Since 1973 production has been reduced as world demand has fallen, a factor that has been experienced by every country included opposite.

Britain, on the other hand, has increased her production by only 50 per cent compared with 1958, the smallest of the increases of the six countries shown here. Her production before the war (1938) and after (1948) was not very different, especially when compared with Japan and West Germany, where production fell substantially between 1938 and 1948 as a result of the war. Since then Germany has continued to increase its production, by 1976 having a larger improvement relative to 1958 than did the United States, although smaller than both Italy and India. Germany's share of world production has improved from 5.6 per cent in 1958 to 8.8 per cent in 1974, whilst Britain's share has fallen from 6.3 per cent to 4.3 per cent and that of the United States from 46.4 per cent to 32.0 per cent.

Data

The diagram opposite represents an index of general industrial production that includes mining, manufacturing, electricity, gas and water. The level of production in 1958 is made equal to 100, with other years being compared with the level in 1958. A figure of 110, therefore, represents an increase of 10 per cent over the 1958 level. Such an index, therefore, considers only changes in levels of production and does not consider absolute values.

Only data for 1938 and 1948 are used prior to 1955, these being joined by dotted lines.

Source

United Nations Statistical Yearbook

Shares of world production

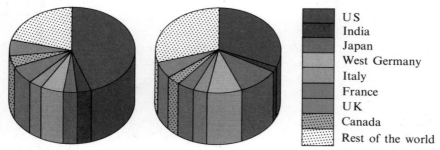

1958   1974

	US
	India
	Japan
	West Germany
	Italy
	France
	UK
	Canada
	Rest of the world

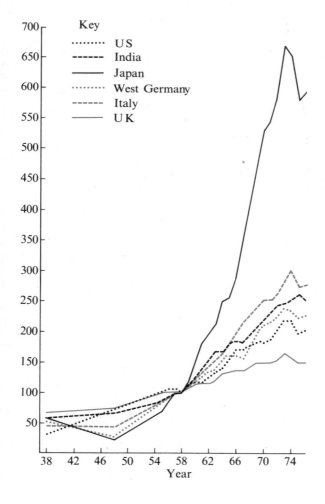

Key

.... US
------ India
——— Japan
.... West Germany
------ Italy
——— UK

Year

5 RATES OF INFLATION

Inflation is one of the most talked about economic topics of today. This is mainly because of the rapid increase in inflation rates at the start of the 1970s, which affected not just Britain but the rest of the world as well. From 1954 up to 1970 there was a general upward trend of inflation rates, from an average rate of about 2 per cent in 1954 to about 5 per cent in 1970, although Britain's rates were slightly higher than this average at 4.7 per cent and 9.4 per cent respectively.

The increase in world prices, due mainly to the oil crisis of the early 1970s, had a dramatic effect on individual nations' economies. The British inflation rate shot up to 24.3 per cent in 1974, as Japan's had during the previous year. India (28.8 per cent), the United States (11.0 per cent), West Germany (7.0 per cent) and Italy (19.1 per cent) also suffered their worst inflation rates in 1973.

Since that time successive prices and/or incomes policies have been implemented in attempts to bring down the rate of inflation, although in Britain and in Italy the rate still remains well above what it was at the end of the 1960s. Japan, West Germany and the United States have been more successful at bringing their rates down to previous levels, although the rises experienced from 1975 to 1976 could suggest that these are only temporary curbs. The new inflation does look as if it is here to stay, and with Governments attempting to bring it down, wage restraint and falling living standards often follow.

Data

The inflation rates shown here are the percentage changes in consumer price indices for different countries. These indices are compiled to show how the cost of consumers' expenditure has changed relative to a base year when the index was equal to 100. The accuracy of such indices is impaired because we do not know exactly what a 'typical' consumer spends his money on, and it is for this reason that the relative weights attributed to different goods are frequently changed as tastes and expenditure patterns change.

Each country's consumer price index, therefore, does include a degree of inaccuracy that is passed on when inflation rates are calculated. This must be borne in mind when comparing the rates opposite.

Source

International Labour Office, Yearbook of Labour Statistics

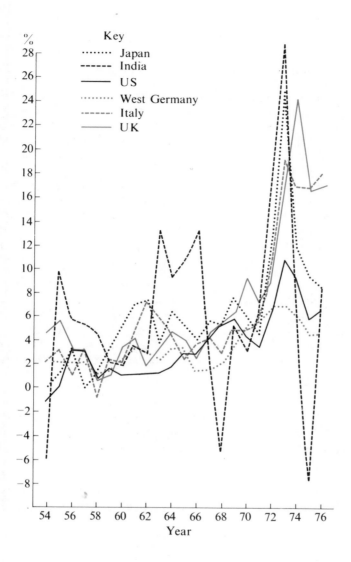

6 PURCHASING POWER OF THE POUND

The previous topic examined the phenomenon of inflation; this present topic describes the effect of that inflation on the purchasing power of the pound. The upper diagram opposite shows how the value of a pound has varied over the years since 1900. In particular, it shows that a 1978 pound was worth just over 5p in terms of its purchasing power relative to a 1900 pound. One of the more interesting features of this diagram is the sharp decline in the value of the pound during, and just after, the First World War (as demand for goods pushed prices up sharply). However, between 1920 and 1935 the value of the pound recovered—rising to a level in 1935 over 70 per cent higher than its level of 1920. Part of this recovery, which of course reflects falling prices, was undoubtedly the consequence of the massive unemployment experienced during these years (the years of the Great Depression).

The Second World War also witnessed sharp falls in the value of the pound. However, unlike the times after the First World War, the following years did not record a subsequent recovery. No doubt this can be attributed partly to the adoption (by postwar governments) of a policy of full employment. As is apparent from the diagram, the value of the pound has declined ever since. This decline has been particularly marked in recent years, as the lower diagram emphasizes. Indeed, by 1978 the pound was worth just 37p in terms of its value eight years before.

Data

The data for the earlier part of the twentieth century is considerably less accurate than that for the latter parts; caution should therefore be exercised in interpreting the figures.

It should, of course, be noted that a declining pound is not necessarily synonomous with declining living standards. On the contrary (as is evidenced elsewhere in this book), living standards have steadily risen during the twentieth century—as earnings have more than kept pace with inflation.

Sources

The British Economy Key Statistics 1900–1970
Economic Trends

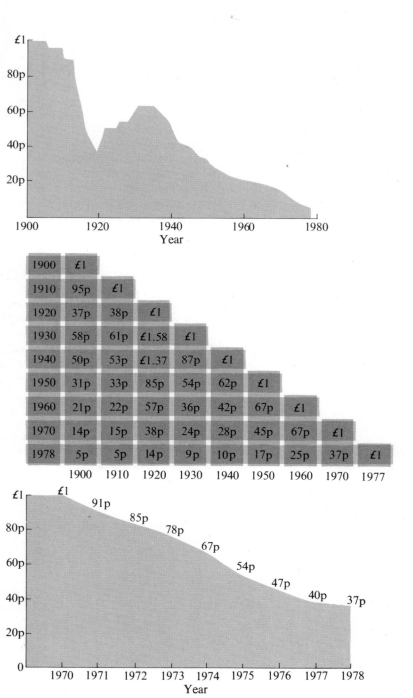

7 PURCHASING POWER OF DIFFERENT CURRENCIES

This topic shows how inflation has affected the purchasing power of foreign currencies as well as the pound. The top diagram opposite demonstrates how different currencies have depreciated since 1955. When we compare the performance of Britain with other countries, we see that by 1975 the pound was worth only 31.8 per cent of its 1954 value, meaning that a sum of money that in 1954 would have bought a whole good would, in 1975, have bought only about a third of that good. India's record of depreciation was even worse than Britain's—its currency slipped to 25.5 per cent of its 1954 value by 1975. Japan too suffered badly, having a purchasing power that was only marginally better than Britain's. West Germany, the United States and, to a lesser extent, Italy were not so badly affected, having purchasing powers in 1975 that were 52.4 per cent, 50.4 per cent and 36.2 per cent, respectively, of their 1954 values.

The lower diagram shows the effect of more recent inflation. This time the purchasing powers of currencies are compared to their 1970 level, which is generally accepted as being just before the world-wide massive inflation began. Britain in this case comes out the worst, with purchasing power being reduced to 54.2 per cent of its 1970 level within five years. The United States and Germany were again the least seriously affected, because of their lower inflation rates, shown in topic 5.

Data

The purchasing powers shown here for different currencies are derived from the consumer price indices which were discussed in topic 5. The problems and inaccuracies that existed in that topic, therefore, are also manifested in this topic.

Source

International Labour Office, Yearbook of Labour Statistics

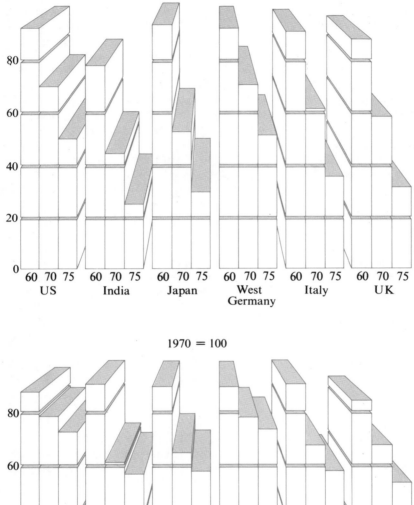

1955 = 100

1970 = 100

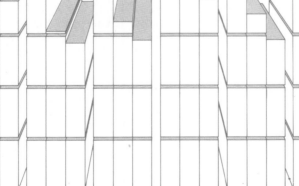

The prices of British exports have risen considerably in recent years, as indeed have the prices of imports into Britain. To assess the *relative* movements of import and export prices (and thus to assess the competitiveness of British exports with those of other countries) a *terms of trade index* is used. This is derived by expressing the export price index as a percentage of the import price index. A rise in this index means that exports are becoming more expensive relative to imports, while a fall implies the opposite. The unfavourable terms of trade that occurred up to 1972 were reversed over the following two years as the terms of trade fell sharply, before rising again to a level of 85 in 1976.

Coupled to the terms of trade are the foreign exchange rates. The exchange rate that is shown opposite concerns the American dollar, showing how many dollars one would get to the pound. From 1954 to 1967 the official exchange rate was held constant, and it was not until the devaluation of the pound on 18 November 1967 that there was any change in its par value. The effect of the devaluation was to give less dollars for a pound. The rate pre-devaluation was $2.80 and $2.40 was the rate immediately following devaluation.

The year 1971 saw new monetary difficulties, with the official limits of exchange rates being suspended in August when the US dollar was no longer convertible into gold, and new limits agreed in December. By June of 1972, however, the Bank of England had suspended the maintenance of dealing within the official limits, and again the value of the pound decreased. Since then, the value of the pound has continued to float down, reaching the rate of $1.80 in 1976 though there was some respite in 1977 and 1978.

Data

The exchange rate figures are averages of daily mean Telegraph rates in London and thus only give a general indication of the exchange rate rather than a sensitive one. If the fluctuations are averaged, the downward movement of the pound relative to the dollar is more easily seen.

Sources

Economic Trends
Annual Abstract of Statistics

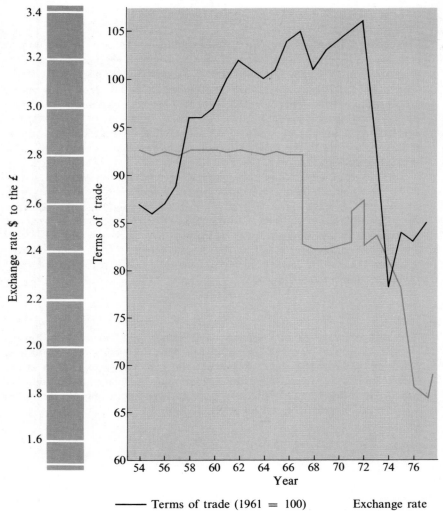

Terms of trade (1961 = 100)　　　　　Exchange rate

9 OFFICIAL RESERVES

The composition of the United Kingdom's reserves has changed remarkably over the last 25 years or so. Gold, the major part (93 per cent) of reserves in 1951, had been reduced to a factor of 21.5 per cent by 1976. Convertible currencies, such as the American dollar, have now taken gold's place with a 61 per cent share of reserves in 1976 compared with an 8 per cent share in 1951. Also included in reserves now are the International Monetary Fund (IMF) Special Drawing Rights and the Reserve Position in the IMF, although reserves did not exist in 1976 for this latter group.

The value of official reserves more than doubled between 1970 and 1971, and has remained at a much higher level than in previous years. Even with this huge increase, it is still possible to relate reserve holdings to the confidence people have in the pound sterling. If there is a lack of confidence in the currency, for example, then money is taken out of sterling, so producing a fall in the reserve stock. On the other hand, reserves increase if money comes into sterling as a result of overseas investors' confidence.

Data

The official reserves that are shown opposite are end-of-year figures published by the Bank of England, and they include a redefinition of reserves made in July 1972 to include the UK reserves position in the IMF. The wide range of transactions and the frequent changing, especially recently, of the value of gold and special drawing rights, does subject the figures to a degree of inaccuracy.

Source

Annual Abstract of Statistics

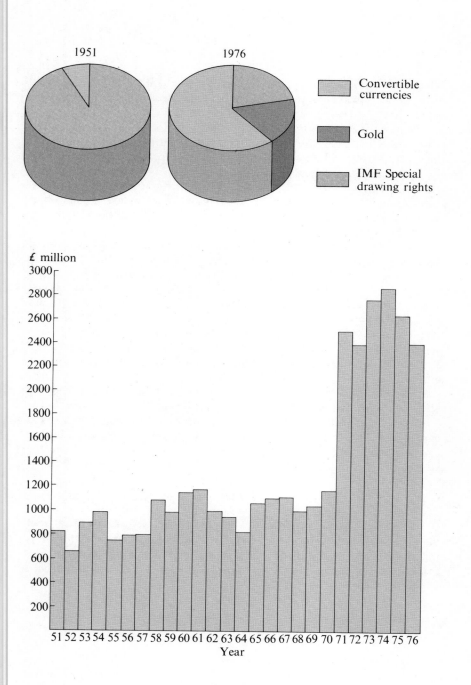

10 BALANCE OF PAYMENTS

The Balance of Payments, like inflation, is a much talked about economic topic; discussion centres round attempts to make receipts coming into the country equal to payments out of the country.

As can be seen from the diagram, Britain has usually had a negative *visible* trade balance. This means that payments for imported goods into this country exceed what foreigners have paid for our exported goods. For every year shown here, however, there has been a positive *invisibles* balance, which incorporates payments made through tourism, insurance, shipping and the like. It is the difference between these two balances that produces the current balance, which is the measure of whether Britain has a surplus or deficit balance.

To give some idea of recent orders of magnitude, it is useful to examine the figures for 1976. Visible credits (that is, exports) totalled £25,416m and visible debits (imports) totalled £28,987m; the difference between these two, a deficit of £3,571m, is the Visible balance (as shown opposite). Invisible credits of £13,838m and debits of £11,672m combined to give a surplus on Invisibles of £2,166m. Thus the current account deficit came to £1,405m. The importance of Invisibles is apparent from this analysis—of all credits (exports), invisibles constituted some 35 per cent, while invisible imports comprised a rather more modest 29 per cent.

Since 1952, the current balance has followed a cyclical pattern centering on zero when Britain has neither a surplus nor a deficit. Recently, however, as a result of the huge increases in oil prices that began in the early 1970s, the current account has moved sharply into deficit. This has led to (moderately successful) governmental attempts to improve it; the advent of North Sea oil has helped in this respect.

Data

Balance of Payments statistics are subject to frequent revisions as new data becomes available, so newly published data are often wildly inaccurate. Although not discussed here, the balance of payments also includes a capital account that is concerned with investment and official transactions.

Sources

United Kingdom Balance of Payments
Economic Trends Annual Supplement

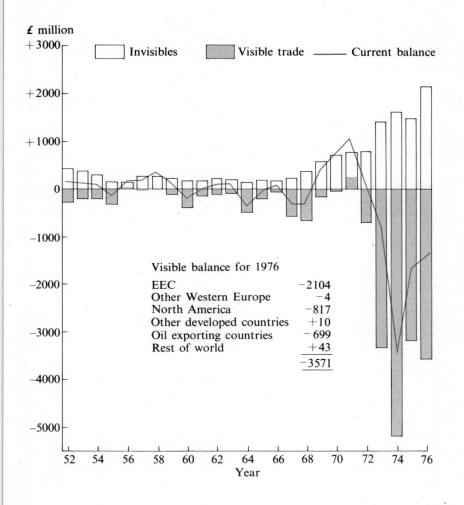

£ million

Invisibles ☐ Visible trade ▨ ── Current balance

Visible balance for 1976

EEC	−2104
Other Western Europe	−4
North America	−817
Other developed countries	+10
Oil exporting countries	−699
Rest of world	+43
	−3571

Year

11 BRITAIN'S SHARE OF WORLD TRADE (GENERAL)

The United Nations collects and publishes much world trade data. From this, percentages of total exports can be calculated for different countries, and it is these that are shown opposite. The figures, however, are not strictly comparable because definitions of trade differ. The United Kingdom, Japan, India, Canada and the USSR all use 'General' trading systems, which include goods that have been imported into customs bonds and re-exported without being cleared for domestic consumption, whereas the other countries shown, with the exception of the United States, use 'Special' trading systems that exclude these above goods. A third category, used by the United States, is for 'semi-Special' trade, which includes exports of domestic produce.

The diagrams opposite show that in 1938 Britain (with 12.1 per cent) and the United States (with 13.5 per cent) had the greatest share of world trade. Britain emerged at the end of the Second World War with a similar share of 11.5 per cent, whereas the United States had pushed its share up to 21.8 per cent. Germany and Japan were badly affected by the war; although no comparisons with West Germany in 1938 can be made because the country then included the East German Democratic Republic and some territories now part of Poland, it is apparent that Germany suffered a similar setback to Japan's, whose share of world trade fell from 4.9 per cent in 1938 to 0.4 per cent in 1948.

By 1963 Britain had slipped sharply behind, managing only a 7.9 per cent share, whereas West Germany had fully recovered from the war and had pushed its share from 1.4 per cent in 1948 to 9.5 per cent in 1963. Japan too had rebuilt its industries, taking its share of exports to 3.5 per cent.

By 1975 Britain's share had fallen still further to 5.0 per cent, and although reductions have also been experienced by the United States (from 15.0 per cent in 1963 to 12.2 per cent in 1975), the British decline remains of the biggest magnitude. On the other extreme, West Germany and, to a larger extent, Japan, continue to expand their share of world trade, with percentages of 10.3 per cent and 6.4 per cent respectively. Also increasing their share are the Middle East countries, who, with the help of their oil, have increased their share from 1.9 per cent in 1938 to 9.2 per cent in 1975.

Source

United Nations Statistical Yearbook, 1976

1938

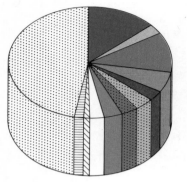

1948

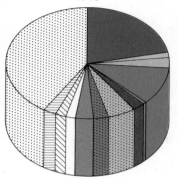

UK
US
Japan
West Germany
Italy
India
France

Canada
Rest of the world
Middle East countries
Belgium & Luxembourg
Netherlands
USSR

1963

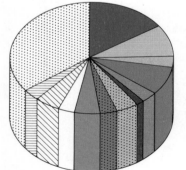

1975

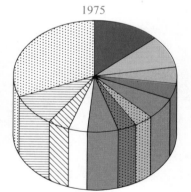

12 BRITAIN'S SHARE OF WORLD TRADE (BROAD GROUPS)

The previous topic showed how Britain has fared in world trade (general). Here we look at broad groupings of trade which demonstrate the specialized nature of world trade in changing economic or physical conditions. In all but the first group—food, beverages and tobacco —Britain's share has declined since 1963. The United States has also experienced diminishing shares.

The largest change comes in the third classification, that of mineral fuels and related materials. Here the oil producing and exporting countries occupy a 63 per cent share of the world market as opposed to 28 per cent in 1963, although this is not strictly comparable with the Middle Eastern figures for that year. For the other classifications the increasing share of world trade gained by European countries is evident. Japan too has advanced, particularly in the chemicals, machinery and transport equipment and other manufactured goods groups. For example, its share of world trade in machinery and transport equipment has increased from 4 per cent in 1963 to 11 per cent in 1975.

These increases by Japan and Western Europe are in direct contrast to British world trade shares, which fell from 11 per cent to 8 per cent for chemicals, from 14 per cent to 7.5 per cent for machinery and transport equipment and from 9 per cent to 6 per cent for other manufactured goods.

Data

The commodity classifications used in the diagrams are from the United Nations Standard International Trade Classification (Revised) (SITC). This, however, excludes trade among mainland China, Mongolia, North Korea and North Vietnam, and between East and West Germany. Not all countries provide information that conforms with this standard classification, so some interpolation must occur, although this should affect only the share attributed to the 'Rest of the World'.

Sources

Monthly Bulletin of Statistics
Yearbook of International Trade Statistics

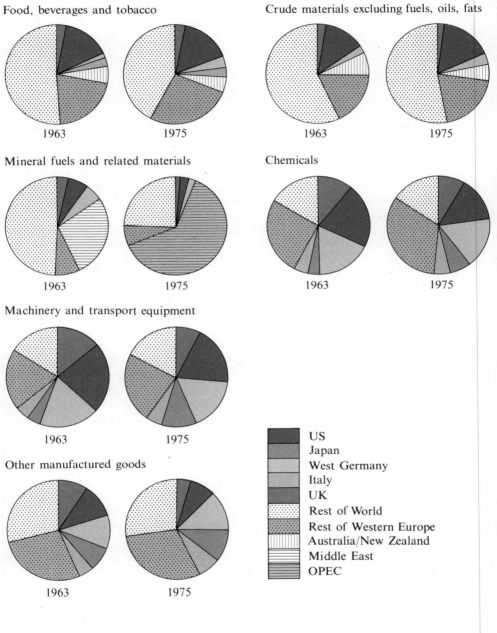

Food, beverages and tobacco

1963   1975

Crude materials excluding fuels, oils, fats

1963   1975

Mineral fuels and related materials

1963   1975

Chemicals

1963   1975

Machinery and transport equipment

1963   1975

Other manufactured goods

1963   1975

US
Japan
West Germany
Italy
UK
Rest of World
Rest of Western Europe
Australia/New Zealand
Middle East
OPEC

13 VOLUME OF BRITAIN'S OVERSEAS TRADE

Britain is a trading nation, primarily importing raw materials and food and exporting manufactured goods, and the volume of trade that goes in and out of the country is considerable. The diagram opposite shows how this volume of exports and imports has grown since 1936. It shows the effect of the Second World War on the level of overseas trade that existed in 1938: there was a sharp decline in trade, especially of exports. These had fallen to a level in 1943 which was 29 per cent that of the 1938 level, with the corresponding trough for imports occurring in 1945 when the level was 62 per cent of the 1938 level.

After the war exports picked up quickly, so that by 1946 they were at their pre-war level. Imports, on the other hand, were much slower, not reaching their 1938 volume again until 1955. Throughout the 1950s and up to the present day, the volume of exports and imports has grown almost hand in hand with increasing world trade generally. With the reduction in the level of world trade in 1974 so too did the volume of British overseas trade decline, reaching a level in 1976 where the volume of exports was over four times the volume in 1938, with the volume of imports being a factor of over two and a half times as big.

Data

The index of the volume of overseas trade is shown using 1938 as the base year. This need not have been a typical year for exports and/or imports, so that comparisons for other years could be biased. Furthermore, the accuracy of trade data for the war years is subject to doubt.

With the constant changing of base years in published data, each new index has to be linked to the old one, again subjecting the final results to a small degree of inaccuracy.

Source

Annual Abstract of Statistics

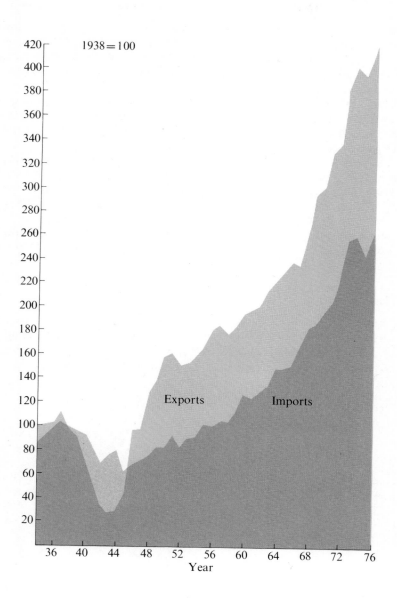

Britain relies heavily on exporting goods, so it seems appropriate to study the composition of her exports. The classifications that are used here are again the United Nations Standard International Trade Classification (Revised), which shows Britain's dependence on the export of manufactured goods. Since 1938 the share of exports attributable to food, beverages and tobacco, crude materials and fuels has remained fairly constant at about 15 per cent. The proportion of chemicals has also remained of similar magnitude, accounting for a share of 11.8 per cent in 1976 compared with 6.3 per cent for the years 1935–38.

Exports of manufactured goods and machinery, however, show the changing pattern of British external trade. Between 1935 and 1938 manufactured goods were the chief export, having a share of total exports of 42.2 per cent. By 1976 though this proportion had slipped to 22.5 per cent, largely due to the advancement of exports of machinery and transport equipment. From a share of UK exports of 19.5 per cent for the period 1935–38 it had reached a share of 39.3 per cent by 1976 to become the main exported commodity in terms of value.

Data

The revision of the classification system has meant that the previous system needed to be updated and corrected, which has led to a small loss of accuracy as the two systems did not overlap. Such discrepancies, however, are small when compared with the overall level of exports.

Source

Annual Abstract of Statistics

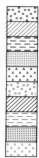

Beverages
Crude materials, inedible
Mineral fuels, lubricants etc.
Animal and vegetable oils and fats
Chemicals
Manufactured goods classified chiefly by material
Machinery and transport equipment
Miscellaneous manufactured goods
Commodities and transactions not classified according to kind
Food and live animals

1935-1938

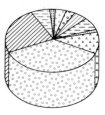

1950

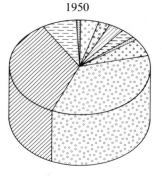

1963

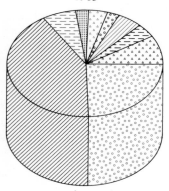

1976

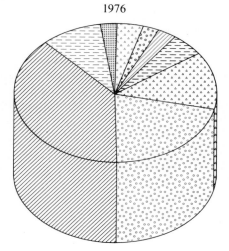

15 DESTINATION AND SOURCE OF BRITAIN'S OVERSEAS TRADE

Joining the European Economic Community (EEC) has had a marked effect on both Britain's imports and exports. In 1976 imports from the EEC accounted for 37 per cent of all our imports, which is over three times the corresponding level of EEC imports in 1951. It means that over half of our imports in 1976 came from the EEC and other Western European countries; this accounts for the loss of imports from Australia and New Zealand. In 1951 Britain imported 11 per cent of its goods from these two countries, but as a result of this move towards European trade the share dropped to 2.3 per cent in 1976.

The significance of the fall in the proportion of imports from the rest of the world is that Britain is importing from a smaller band of countries who are able to supply an increasing share of her needs. This is apparent too when we consider exports. Here, Australia and New Zealand have suffered similarly, while the oil exporting countries and other members of the EEC benefited to the extent that the proportion of Britain's exports going to the EEC rose from 10.4 per cent in 1951 to 36 per cent in 1976. North America received a slightly larger share of Britain's exports, as did the rest of Western Europe, meaning that over half of Britain's exports in 1976 went to Europe.

Data

The figures for the Middle East and OPEC countries are not strictly comparable, but they have had to have been used here due to the revision of published data. It should be noted also that the EEC was officially termed the European Coal and Steel Community in 1951, although membership did not change until Britain, Denmark and Ireland joined in 1973.

Centrally planned economies refer to the USSR, Poland, the German Democratic Republic, Czechoslovakia, and Rumania. The abbreviation OPEC refers to the oil producing and exporting developing countries, and *not* to the economic organization which used to use the same initials.

Source

Annual Abstract of Statistics

US
Japan
Rest of the world
Middle East
South Africa

Centrally planned economics
Australia
Rest of Western Europe
EEC
OPEC countries

Imports

1976

1951

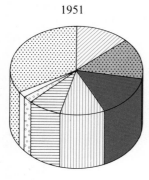

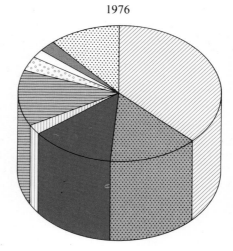

Exports

1976

1951

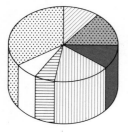

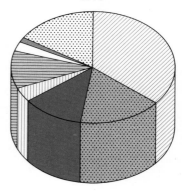

In 1958 Britain had the highest value of exports per head of population among the countries shown, demonstrating further that she relies heavily on overseas trade. Within ten years, however, Britain's commanding lead had been cut down by all countries with the exception of India. West Germany had in fact just overtaken Britain as she continued to rebuild her industries after the Second World War. Japan, West Germany and Italy all more than doubled their exports per head within that ten-year period, while Britain could manage only a 12 per cent increase.

Seven years later, in 1975, Germany had far outstripped the others, even though the increase in world trade had increased most countries' exports. Japan again doubled its 1968 figure, while foreign trade for Italy and the United States grew faster than Britain's. However, Britain still had the second highest value of exports per head of population.

Data

The population figures used in these tables are United Nations estimates of mid-year population numbers. The fact that they are estimates, and thus subject to a high risk of inaccuracy—especially in the case of India—leads to reservations about the results. Moreover, each currency has been converted to a common denominator, American dollars, so providing yet more room for inaccuracy.

Sources

United Nations Statistical Yearbook
United Nations Demographic Yearbook

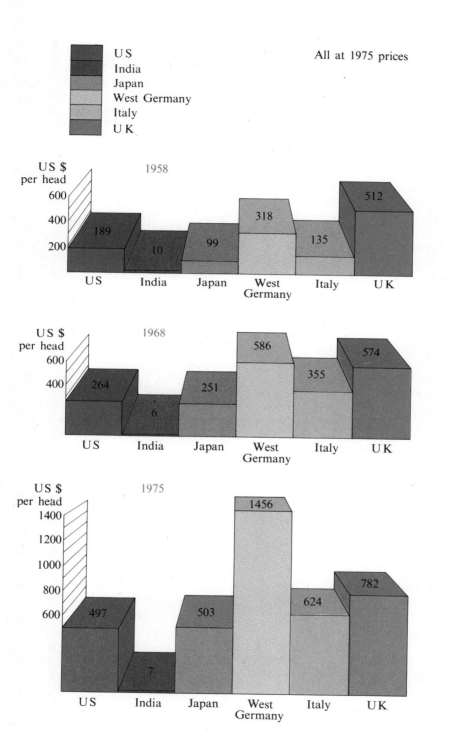

17 GROSS DOMESTIC PRODUCT (GENERAL)

Gross Domestic Product, as its name implies, is a measure of the total domestic production of goods and services within a given time period. As such, it is a crude indicator of the well-being of a country: other things being equal, if the country's Gross Domestic Product (GDP) rises, then there is a higher volume of goods and services to share out amongst the inhabitants of the country. (It is only a *crude* measure of well-being, since factors other than the volume of goods and services affect welfare; for example, if the extra output could be obtained only at the expense of spoiling a large area of the Lake District, say, then strong doubts about the wisdom of producing that extra amount would be voiced!)

The upper graph opposite shows how GDP has moved over the post-war period. As is clear from this graph, the general picture is one of steadily rising output with occasional 'hiccups'—the latest being that of the 1975 'mini-recession'. During the period portrayed, GDP, measured at constant 1970 prices (which is a volume measure—ignoring the effects of inflation) rose from £23,474m in 1948 to £48,394m in 1976; thus total output more than doubled over this 29-year period. (This increase may usefully be put into perspective by noting that in the 49 years between 1900 and 1948, GDP rose by just under 60 per cent; thus post-war growth has been at a higher rate.)

As will be discussed in more detail in topic 19, there are three alternative methods by which statisticians at the Central Statistical Office measure GDP. Two of these methods—those using output and income data (the third method uses expenditure data)—are portrayed over the period from 1970 in the lower graph. As is apparent from this graph, quarterly fluctuations in GDP can be considerable, yet a relatively smooth trend is obtained in the annual data.

Data

Gross Domestic Product can be calculated at 'market prices', or at 'factor cost'. The former is calculated by aggregating all goods and services at their market prices, while the latter allows for indirect taxes (such as VAT), and subsidies. Thus, by subtracting the net total of indirect taxes from GDP at market prices, one arrives at GDP at factor cost—this is the figure that is paid out to factors in the form of incomes.

Source

Economic Trends Annual Supplement

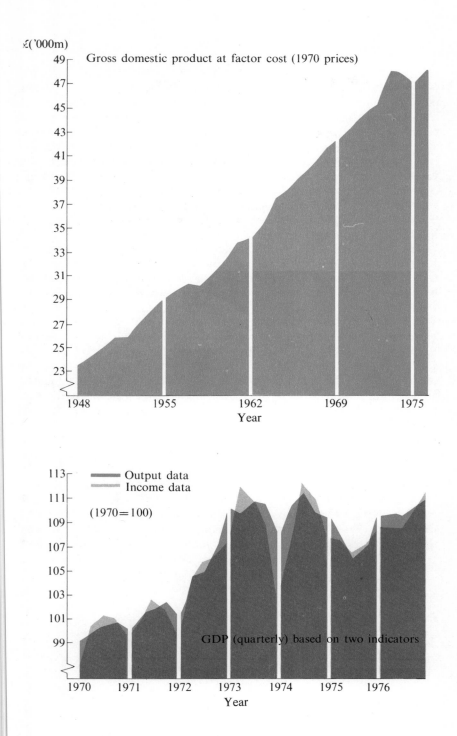

£('000m)

Gross domestic product at factor cost (1970 prices)

Year

Output data
Income data

(1970=100)

GDP (quarterly) based on two indicators

Year

One possible way of measuring GDP is to consider the income components, and it is on this that the analysis will now concentrate. There are four such components shown in the diagram; their names are self-explanatory, but is is worth remembering that Gross Trading profits refers to gross profit before allowing for depreciation and stock appreciation. The diagrams show total domestic income; in order to calculate gross domestic product at factor cost, one simply subtracts the value of stock appreciation for each particular year. (Usually stock appreciation is only some 2 per cent or less of GDP, although in recent years its relative importance has increased somewhat.) The component labelled 'other income' includes such things as income from rent, and income from self-employment.

The time-series shows the movement of total domestic income from 1967 to 1976 in real terms, and the graph portrays a general increasing trend over these years. But the graph does not give any information on how income is broken down—so for this reason, the pie-charts below were drawn.

The size of the pie-charts is proportional to the total domestic income it represents. It is interesting to compare the proportion of total domestic income each component constitutes, and how these proportions change. Comparing 1976 to 1948, income from employment constitutes a larger proportion of the total, as does gross trading surplus of general government enterprises and public corporations, but the proportion of gross trading profits of companies has declined. The proportion of 'other income' has remained virtually constant between the two years.

Data

The original data for total domestic income, and its components, were published in current prices. Therefore, it has to be converted into real terms by using a price index. Many different price indices could be used, but the one which was chosen was an implied index of total home costs derived from expenditure data—this is published in the same source, and is the one used by the Central Statistical Office.

Source

Economic Trends Annual Supplement, 1977

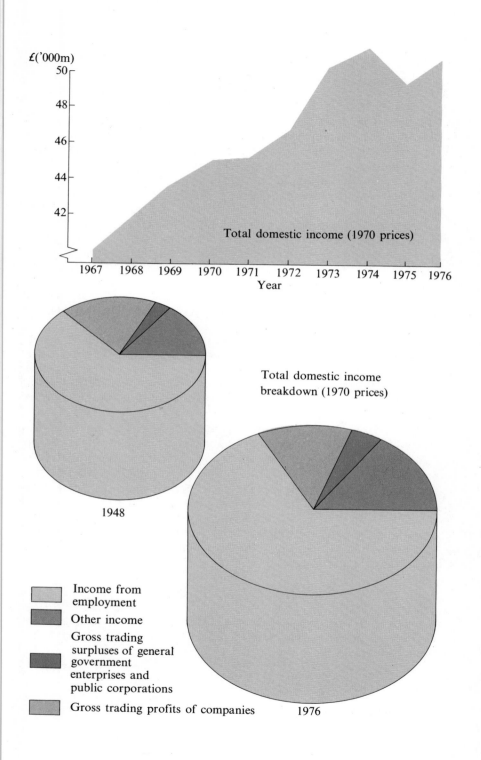

£('000m)

Total domestic income (1970 prices)

Year

Total domestic income
breakdown (1970 prices)

1948

1976

Income from
employment

Other income

Gross trading
surpluses of general
government
enterprises and
public corporations

Gross trading profits of companies

At this point, it may be useful to make explicit what has been implicit so far: that the activity of the economy, as measured by Gross Domestic Product, can in theory be calculated in three different ways—all of which should give the same answer. The three different ways are as follows:
(1) by adding up all the incomes received by people working for the UK;
(2) by adding up the amount spent by everyone on UK goods; and
(3) by adding up the amount of output produced in the UK.
Why the three measures should in theory be the same is simple: whatever is produced must be paid for, and whatever one person spends must become some other person's income. (Although errors in data collection mean that the three never exactly coincide, the fact that they should provides a useful check to statisticians working in the Central Statistical Office.)

The previous topic, 18, examined the components making up the income-based measure of GDP; the next, 20, examines the output components; in this present topic, the expenditure components are examined.

In the diagram opposite, the items to the right of the vertical line measure 'positive' expenditure components, while those to the left are 'negative' components. (Imports are clearly a negative component since money spent on imports into the UK contributes to the GDP of foreign countries and not to that of the UK; adjustment to factor cost represents the amount 'creamed off' by the government).

As is apparent from the picture, consumer spending is by far the largest component of total expenditure—amounting to some 73.2 per cent in 1976. In 1976, the second largest component was exports, amounting to 31.8 per cent of GDP, though imports of 29.4 per cent largely offset this. Capital formation accounted for 19.9 per cent of the total. The percentage of GDP spent by general government has risen in recent years; by 1976 it had reached 22.8 per cent after having touched 20.7 per cent during the early part of the 1970s. Nevertheless, these shares remain well below the 25.4 per cent to 28.9 per cent range recorded during the period 1948 to 1955.

Data

Because of the small size of the expenditure component 'value of physical increase in stocks and work-in-progress' it was combined with fixed capital formation.

Source

Economic Trends Annual Supplement

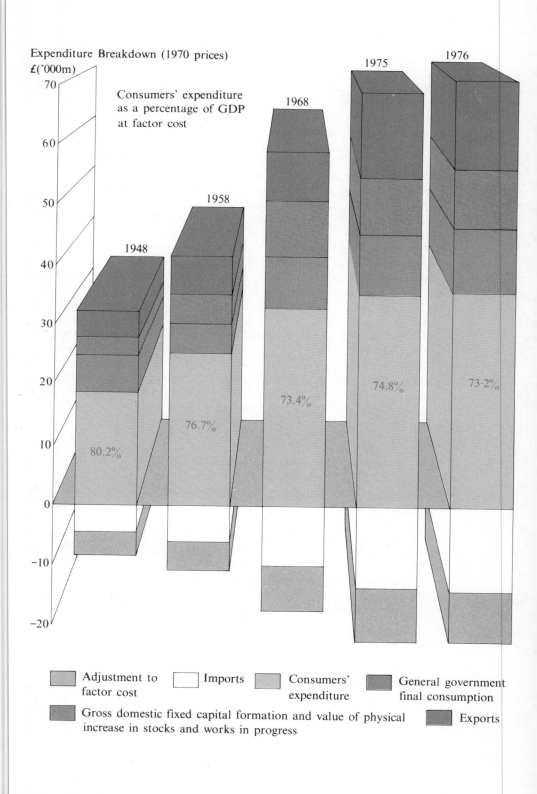

Expenditure Breakdown (1970 prices)
£('000m)

Consumers' expenditure
as a percentage of GDP
at factor cost

1948   80.2%

1958   76.7%

1968   73.4%

1975   74.8%

1976   73·2%

Adjustment to factor cost

Imports

Consumers' expenditure

General government final consumption

Gross domestic fixed capital formation and value of physical increase in stocks and works in progress

Exports

In this final topic on gross domestic product, we will analyse GDP in yet another way—by examining the output components, such as manufacturing, construction and agriculture. It is interesting to consider how various components have fluctuated over time and some possible explanations for these fluctuations.

The large pie chart shows individual output components of GDP, making it possible to identify the more influential components of output. The smaller pie chart takes the most influential component of output— namely, industrial production—and shows *its* components. It will be noticed that manufacturing is a very large component of industrial production —constituting very nearly three quarters of total industrial output.

The second part of the diagram, the time-series, shows the performance of the components of total industrial production over the years from 1965 to 1976. The 'spiderlike' diagram has one eye-catching feature—the plunge of mining and quarrying. The mining industry has been on the decline over the years; coal used to be more important than it is today. Now, new sources of energy are becoming more powerful: electricity, and particularly North Sea Gas, are the obvious examples. Indeed, the gas, electricity, and water component has shown a steady growth over time, and this emphasizes their increasing importance in the modern world. The manufacturing and construction components show a steady growth up to the mid-1970s, and then they both declined —construction much more so than manufacturing.

Data

One rather surprising feature of the large pie chart is the size of the segment labelled 'Other Services'. It is so large because many categories have been grouped together—for example, social services, other public services, and other service industries. *Individually*, each of these components constitutes a very small proportion of the total, but altogether they make up a substantial proportion. The two pie charts bear the correct relationships to each other in size—that is, the size of the pie is proportional to the quantity it represents.

Finally, it should be noted that all the time-series in the 'spiderlike' diagram are based on 100 in the year 1970. This graph, therefore, shows only *relative* movements in output.

Sources

National Income and Expenditure, 1966–76
Economic Trends Annual Supplement, 1977

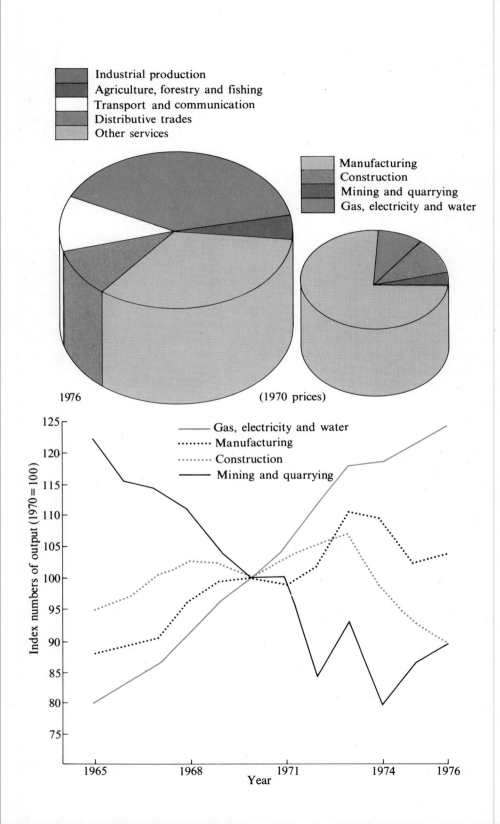

Industrial production
Agriculture, forestry and fishing
Transport and communication
Distributive trades
Other services

Manufacturing
Construction
Mining and quarrying
Gas, electricity and water

1976   (1970 prices)

Gas, electricity and water
Manufacturing
Construction
Mining and quarrying

Index numbers of output (1970 = 100)

Year

21 INTERNATIONAL TRANSACTIONS

This topic examines two of the most important components of expenditure-data based GDP: exports and imports of goods and services. Exports are a positive contributor to Gross Domestic Product, in that increases in exports lead to increases in GDP (because foreigners are demanding British goods, and the money they pay for them becomes income for British residents). On the other hand, imports detract from GDP, in that increases in imports lead to *decreases* in GDP (because we are demanding foreign goods, and the money we pay for them becomes income for foreigners).

The top graph is a time-series plot of exports and imports in volume (that is, real) terms. As is apparent, considerable growth occurred over the period portrayed. (Indeed, exports in 1976 were over three-a-half times the volume recorded in 1948. Imports increased more than three-fold over this period.)

The 'bar chart' at the bottom of the page presents, in greater close-up, the difference between the export and import volumes over the later part of the period. When imports exceed exports, the difference is negative, and is portrayed as a bar below zero; when exports exceed imports, the difference is positive, and is portrayed as a bar above zero. As can be seen, the net difference is negative for most of the 1960s, though after devaluation in 1967, a clear improvement is apparent.

Data

It is important to note that these figures are in real terms; that is, they represent the volume of imports and exports as given in 1970 prices. The difference between exports and imports is, therefore, *not* the current account balance as conventionally understood (which is the difference between exports and imports in money terms, and is portrayed in topic 10). Rather, it represents what the current account balance *would have been* if prices had been at their 1970 levels throughout the period.

Source

Economic Trends Annual Supplement, 1977

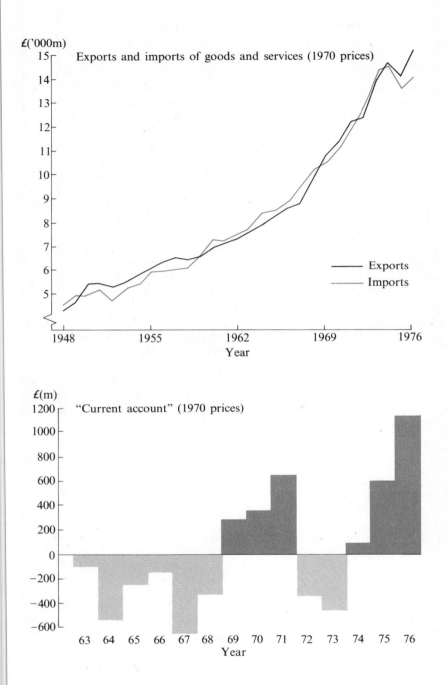

£('000m)

Exports and imports of goods and services (1970 prices)

Exports

Imports

Year

£(m)

"Current account" (1970 prices)

Year

22 CAPITAL FORMATION BY INDUSTRY

Capital formation is another important component of expenditure-data based GDP. Capital formation represents additions to the nation's stock of real capital (a more detailed definition will be given in the next topic). Since a greater output of goods and services can usually be obtained with a greater stock of capital (even though the number of workers remains the same), it follows that capital formation is vital if the output of the economy is to grow.

The time-series graph at the top of the page opposite shows how the volume of capital formation in aggregate has moved over the period 1963 to 1976. Evidently real growth took place during all but the last two years of this period, although the rate of growth varied considerably. At the peak level of 1974, the total volume of investment in the UK was somewhat over one-and-a-half times its 1963 level. The reductions in capital spending recorded for 1975 and 1976 were the consequences of the 'mini recession' induced by the oil-price rises of 1973.

The pie charts show the composition of aggregate capital formation for two years—1963 and 1976. The area of the pies is proportional to the total investment. As is apparent from these charts, the agriculture, forestry and fishing sector has decreased in relative importance (as far as capital formation is concerned) between 1963 and 1976, along with the composite group, gas, electricity, water, etc. Service industries have grown in relative importance over this period. This fact reflects the growing importance of the service sector in the UK. (Indeed, this is a general phenomenon: as a country gets richer, a greater proportion of its activity becomes concentrated in the service sectors.)

Source

National Income and Expenditure

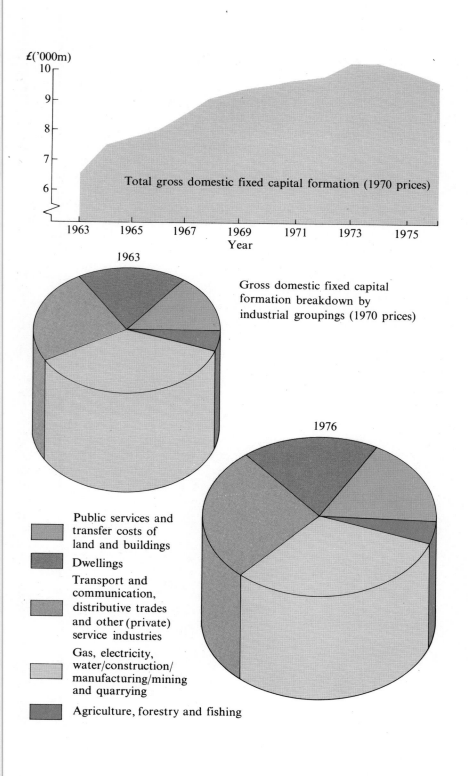

£('000m)

Total gross domestic fixed capital formation (1970 prices)

Year

1963

Gross domestic fixed capital
formation breakdown by
industrial groupings (1970 prices)

1976

Public services and
transfer costs of
land and buildings

Dwellings

Transport and
communication,
distributive trades
and other (private)
service industries

Gas, electricity,
water/construction/
manufacturing/mining
and quarrying

Agriculture, forestry and fishing

23 CAPITAL FORMATION BY ASSET

The previous topic examined how individual industries contributed to total capital formation—that is, it presented an *industrial* breakdown of investment. In contrast, this topic looks at an *asset* breakdown of capital formation—that is, it examines investment in different types of asset.

Capital formation is simply investment in real assets, that is, additions to the stock of real capital. Gross capital formation includes depreciation —repairs and maintenance expenditure, while net capital formation excludes them.

What does economic theory suggest about the criteria used to determine increases in the stock of real capital? First, an increase in consumer spending will stimulate production; this can be achieved by employing the spare capacity at first, but later, a more intensive use of capital will be needed. Second, if the rate of interest falls, businessmen may tend to invest more in plant and machinery, for example, as loans become cheaper. Both of these criteria may be subject to lagged effects: interest rate this year may influence investment next year. Third, if company profits increase, it may be a sign of the economy's becoming more healthy, and hence prospects for the future will be good, thus stimulating investment. Fourth, the government can offer firms incentives to invest; for example, they could lower taxation. The government can also undertake investment itself.

The time series shows the growth of gross domestic fixed capital formation, while the pie chart breaks the aggregate into its various components. This gives some idea of how influential various components are in respect to the aggregate, and it is obvious that plant and machinery, new buildings, and works are very important components.

The bar charts break down dwellings into private and public sectors, and the movement of these with respect to each other is interesting. The trend for private dwellings is a definite decrease, while the trend for public dwellings is an increase.

Source

Economic Trends Annual Supplement, 1977

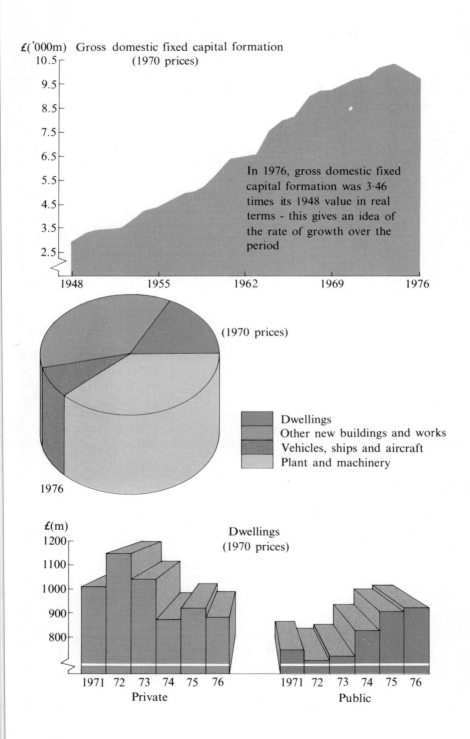

£('000m) Gross domestic fixed capital formation
(1970 prices)

10.5
9.5
8.5
7.5
6.5
5.5
4.5
3.5
2.5

In 1976, gross domestic fixed
capital formation was 3·46
times its 1948 value in real
terms - this gives an idea of
the rate of growth over the
period

1948   1955   1962   1969   1976

(1970 prices)

Dwellings
Other new buildings and works
Vehicles, ships and aircraft
Plant and machinery

1976

£(m)   Dwellings
1200   (1970 prices)
1100
1000
900
800

1971 72 73 74 75 76   1971 72 73 74 75 76
Private   Public

Personal income allocation can be divided into several categories, shown in the pie chart opposite. Virtually three-quarters of income is used up buying goods and services for immediate or future consumption (that is, consumers' expenditure). Taxation and national insurance contributions constitute about one-seventh of total personal income, while the remaining segment represents savings. In other words, income is either spent, saved or taken away by the government. Once the government has taken the direct taxes and national insurance contributions from the total income, the residual is known as personal disposable income—the amount available for consumption and saving.

The time-series graph shows the movement of disposable income; in real terms, as expected, there has been a fairly steady growth. For example, in 1975 personal disposable income was 2.2 times its 1948 value in real terms. Reference to the disposable income per head tables will suggest that disposable income *per head* took approximately from 1948 to 1976 to double in value.

Data

It is vitally important here to remember that the figures relate to the whole country. Thus, while *on average*, one-seventh of personal income goes on taxation and national insurance contributions, some people pay a considerably greater proportion, while others pay a considerably smaller proportion. Of particular importance in this latter category are most old-age pensioners and other social security recipients. The saving ratio and consumption ratio are percentages of total disposable income saved or spent.

Sources

Economic Trends Annual Supplement
National Income and Expenditure

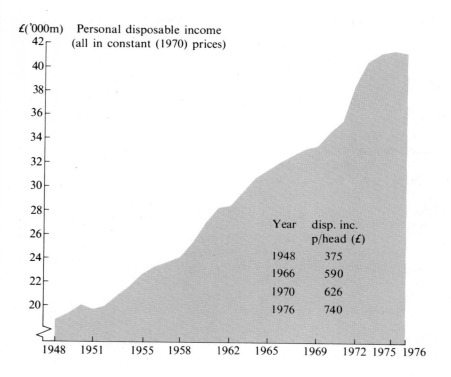

£('000m) Personal disposable income
(all in constant (1970) prices)

Year	disp. inc. p/head (£)
1948	375
1966	590
1970	626
1976	740

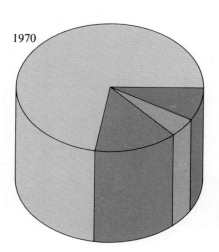

1970

Year	Saving ratio	Consumption ratio
1966	9.1	90.9
1967	8.5	91.5
1968	7.9	92.1
1969	8.1	91.9
1970	8.9	91.1
1971	8.5	91.5
1972	10.5	89.5
1973	11.7	88.3
1974	14.1	85.9
1975	15.3	84.7
1976	14.6	85.4

Saving
Consumers' expenditure
NI contributions
UK taxes on income and transfers abroad

The economic activities of general government can be classified into three broad categories: (1) consumption expenditure (that is, spending on goods and services for current consumption); (2) capital expenditure (that is, spending on buildings, machinery and other capital equipment); and (3) transfer payments (that is, the transferring of purchasing power from one group of citizens to another group—most notable in this category are social security payments of one form or another).

The first of these three categories—namely, consumption expenditure—is portrayed in the pictures opposite. Although this does not indicate the full extent of government intervention in the economy, it does give some idea of relative movements. Moreover, it is the largest component in general, and is usually more accurately measured than the other two components. The diagrams, which portray general government consumption expenditure as a percentage of Gross National Product, show in general a rising share of output spent on current consumption by the governments of the countries represented. Japan, however, is a notable exception to this general trend.

Estimates of the *sum* of the three components (mentioned in the first paragraph above) as a *percentage of National Income* are provided, for OECD countries, in the book by Nutter. These estimates show that between 1958 and 1973 the percentage in West Germany rose from 42 per cent to 50 per cent; in Italy, it rose from 36 per cent to 49 per cent; in Japan from 18 per cent to 27 per cent; in the UK from 39 per cent to 50 per cent; and in the US from 36 per cent to 40 per cent. (1974 figures for West Germany, Japan and the UK were 54 per cent, 29 per cent and 55 per cent respectively; those for Italy and the US were not given.) Although the absolute sizes of these percentages should be interpreted with caution (see below), the general trend of increasing government intervention in many major countries is apparent.

Data

As Nutter remarks, the figures in the third paragraph above are not necessarily good indicators of the extent of government intervention in the economy; indeed these percentages overstate '. . . the command over use of resources exercised by the government . . .'—the degree of overstatement depending on the importance of transfer payments. In particular, it is vital to note that this 'percentage' could well rise to over 100 per cent '. . . even though ultimate use of resources would still be substantially determined by private spending'. A good indicator of the 'size of the public sector' remains to be determined.

Sources

United Nations Statistical Yearbooks
Nutter, G. Warren, *Growth of Government in the West*.

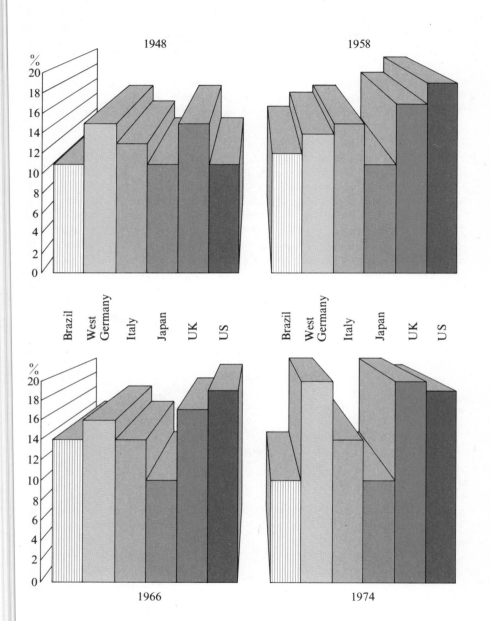

The two pie charts opposite portray the growth in real terms of public expenditure over a ten-year period. As can be seen, there has been an increase in expenditure on all the items shown, but this increase has taken place at different rates. Some items have altered in their significance in proportional terms; they do not have the same size slice in both diagrams. Of these, perhaps military defence is the most striking. From a fairly large slice in 1965 it has shrunk to a much smaller size in 1975. Social services have increased their share slightly, this increase mainly being taken up by education.

The various residual categories, which are clearly growing in relative importance, cover a multitude of items. The 'other' in the social services includes personal social services, school meals, milk and welfare foods; the 'other' in the housing and environmental services includes water, sewerage, public health services, land drainage and coast protection, and parks and pleasure grounds; and the other 'others' covers a variety of items including civil defence, external relations, research, libraries, museums and arts, prisons, parliament and law courts, the fire service and finance and tax collection.

The public authorities expenditure covers a wide variety of items. The main reasons why these items are predominantly state-controlled is either because of a belief and desire that all members of society enjoy their benefits regardless of their wealth (health and education and housing) or because, as in the case of the police and military defence, of their potential power base or because the private sector on its own would not provide them or would charge high prices for their use (roads and environmental services and some social services). In cases such as these there are few arguments against state intervention. What becomes debatable is whether the state should control these sectors to the exclusion of private organizations. This is the case with education and health care where much discussion arises.

Data

The data is originally given in market prices for each year. An index has been applied in order that the areas of each circle may be portrayed as proportional in real terms:

Source

Annual Abstract of Statistics, 1976

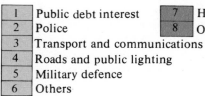

1	Public debt interest
2	Police
3	Transport and communications
4	Roads and public lighting
5	Military defence
6	Others

Total housing and
environmental services

| 7 | Housing |
| 8 | Other |

Total social services

9	Social security benefits
10	National health service
11	Education
12	Other

1965

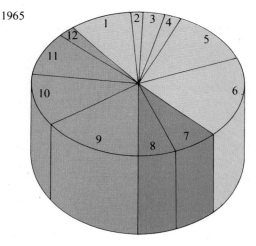

1975

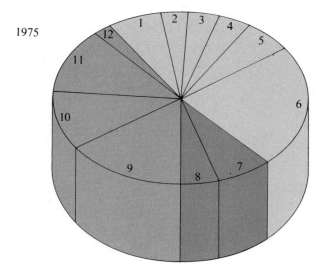

The topmost bar chart shows a comparison of the percentage of total expenditure that the governments of five countries devote to education. Brazil devotes the largest proportion, possibly because it is a developing country with lower basic standards and a greater need to educate its population. With the other countries standards are higher and so the emphasis is on other areas.

The make-up of the population is also important. If a large proportion of a country's inhabitants are of school-age then there will be greater expenditure on schooling than on old-age allowances because of the number of individuals in each age group. This can be seen most dramatically for the years following the wars. The post-war baby boom increased the need for nurseries; as the babies grow older then there are successive needs for increased schooling, jobs and finally old-age care. This is the case unless other wars or disasters take their toll of the population.

The middle diagram shows changes in the proportion spent in the UK by the public authorities on education over a fifteen-year period. The general trend has been an increase in the importance of education. This is partly because of the diminishing provision of education by the private sector.

The bottom bar chart shows the increase in real terms at 1970 prices of expenditure in the UK. Even though proportionally there was a dramatic fall in 1973 and 1974 there was not a fall in real terms. 1975 saw an increase in proportional and real terms yet again.

The pie chart represents the complete breakdown of expenditure. As is expected current expenditure takes the largest share. Capital expenditure also, surprisingly, takes a fairly large slice (compared with capital expenditure on military defence.)

Data

The only major problem with the data applies to the bottom bar chart. Here a general price index has been applied where ideally an index relating to education alone would be used. An education index would take into account only such items as the price of books, teachers' salaries, etc., while the general index is concerned with all items of consumer expenditure. Unfortunately, such specialized indices are rarely available.

Sources

UN Statistical Yearbook, 1975
Annual Abstract of Statistics, 1969 and 1976
National Income and Expenditure, 1966–68, 1965–75 and 1976

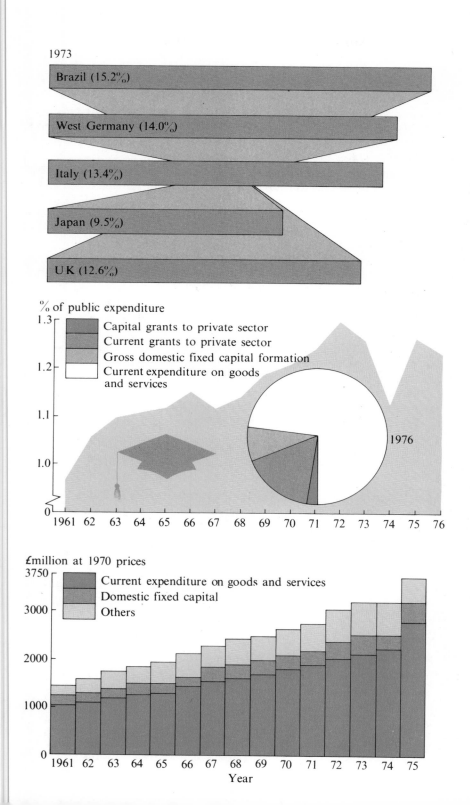

1973

Brazil (15.2%)

West Germany (14.0%)

Italy (13.4%)

Japan (9.5%)

U K (12.6%)

% of public expenditure

1.3

■ Capital grants to private sector
■ Current grants to private sector
■ Gross domestic fixed capital formation
□ Current expenditure on goods
and services

1.2

1.1

1.0

1976

0

1961 62 63 64 65 66 67 68 69 70 71 72 73 74 75 76

£million at 1970 prices

3750

■ Current expenditure on goods and services
■ Domestic fixed capital
□ Others

3000

2000

1000

0

1961 62 63 64 65 66 67 68 69 70 71 72 73 74 75

Year

The top diagram shows how little the percentage of public expenditure on the National Health Service has altered over the last fifteen years. There has been a slight rise since 1968 from 8.7 per cent to only 10.1 per cent. The fact that the proportional expenditure on the NHS has remained much the same means that in real terms it has grown at much the same rate as total public authorities expenditure.

1973 saw the same fall in proportional terms which applied to education but to a far less dramatic extent. This fall applies to the social services so implying that greater emphasis was being placed on other items within government influence.

In real terms expenditure was still growing, as it has done during the whole period shown. In fifteen years real expenditure on the NHS has nearly doubled and expenditure on education has tripled. One possible reason for this difference in growth is that the provision of health care has in recent history been almost entirely supplied by the state. Within the sphere of education, there has been an area controlled by the private sector. The state could, therefore, if it wished or felt it necessary, take over this area.

The pie chart depicts the usual case that current expenditure takes up the majority of total expenditure. There is also a fairly large share devoted to capital formation. This is not surprising, since medical equipment is generally expensive. Over the period shown this capital expenditure in real terms has had a varied experience. Some years there has been lower expenditure than before. There is still, however, a general growth.

Data

Much the same comments apply to the bar chart showing expenditure in real terms as applied to that on education. The problem of indices is the same.

No international comparisons are given because of the difficulty in comparing expenditure on health: acquiring the data for other countries in the necessary form. Provision of health care is not always predominantly supplied by the state and so comparisons would therefore show a wide fluctuation.

Sources

Annual Abstract of Statistics, 1969 and 1976
National Income and Expenditure, 1966–68, 1965–75 and 1976

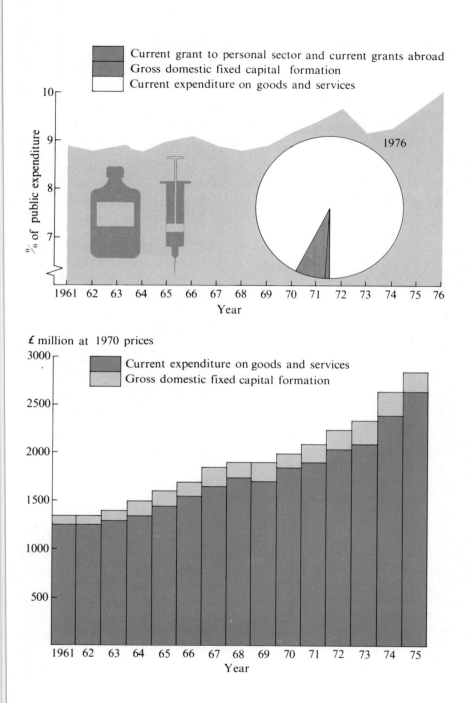

Current grant to personal sector and current grants abroad
Gross domestic fixed capital formation
Current expenditure on goods and services

% of public expenditure

10
9
8
7

1961 62 63 64 65 66 67 68 69 70 71 72 73 74 75 76

Year

1976

£ million at 1970 prices

3000

Current expenditure on goods and services
Gross domestic fixed capital formation

2500

2000

1500

1000

500

1961 62 63 64 65 66 67 68 69 70 71 72 73 74 75

Year

The top right table shows how, across the five countries, the proportion of public expenditure (but see *Data*) spent on national defence has fallen from 1958 to 1974. The actual size of the figures is misleading, for the reasons given below. What is clear is that there has been a general decline in the importance of defence in all countries. The first diagram shows in greater detail this decline.

From 1962 to 1969 there was a sharp, constant drop in the proportion spent; this fall was continued after 1970. It would be expected that the proportional expenditure on National Defence would decline after a war but the period shown is a decade and a half after the end of the Second World War.

The main reason for this continued fall in percentage of expenditure is that Britain no longer plays a large military role in the world. What responsibilities it does hold are mainly in the NATO and Ireland. The recent threat to Belize is worth mentioning if only because it is Britain's one possession on the American continent. (As readers may remember, Guatemala threatened a takeover in 1977.) There is little desire on behalf of an American colony (unlike the situation two hundred years ago) to see the British depart so there is still a need to finance a military presence.

In real terms there has been no smooth pattern throughout the whole of the past fifteen years. From 1961 to 1967 there was a general if modest increase but this was followed by a severe drop in 1969, as shown in the bar graph. Since then there has been a gradual increase again but this has yet to reach the 1967 level of expenditure.

Another unusual aspect of military defence is the breakdown of expenditure, shown in the pie chart. A very small proportion is devoted to capital formation. It would be expected that military installations are at least as expensive as hospitals or schools. It is therefore reasonable to conclude that very few are being built.

Data

The actual figures in the table cannot be compared in terms of size because they are not all percentages of the same totals. For Brazil and the USA the percentages are of federal expenditure on military defence. These figures are, therefore, higher than the others. West Germany has only figures for current expenditure (excluding capital formation) as a percentage of combined public authorities expenditure so these figures are low. Japan and the UK are complete expenditure as a percentage of total public authorities expenditure.

Sources

UN Statistical Yearbooks, 1962, 1975 and 1976
Annual Abstract of Statistics, 1969 and 1976
National Income and Expenditure, 1966–68, 1965–75 and 1976

Public expenditure on defence %

	Brazil	West Germany	Japan	UK	US
1958	27.5	7.1	11.3	24.7	53.4
1974	14.0	6.7	5.6	9.9	29.3

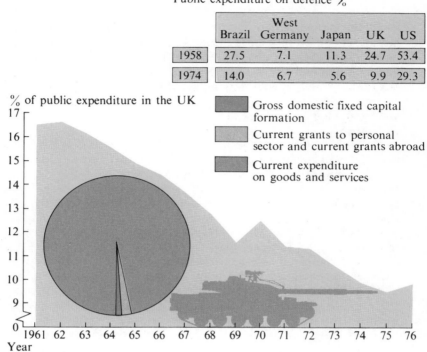

% of public expenditure in the UK

Gross domestic fixed capital formation

Current grants to personal sector and current grants abroad

Current expenditure on goods and services

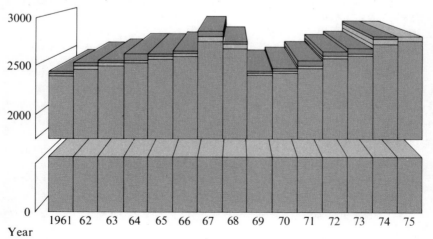

£millions in 1970 prices

When the amounts of ground-force manpower for the Warsaw Pact and NATO countries in Central Europe are compared, we see that the numbers are nearly equivalent for the two sides: NATO have a total of 823,000 men and the Warsaw Pact 899,000 men. Excluded from the NATO total are French troops in France and Danish troops in Denmark, which could be used in the event of a war in Central Europe between East and West. Neither side would be at an advantage in terms of the size of their armies.

The lower illustration opposite shows that, in 1976, NATO were outnumbered two to one for numbers of combat aircraft: the Warsaw Pact had some 3,000 aircraft as opposed to NATO's 1,436. Since 1976, the position has worsened considerably: the present ratio probably being over three to one. Because aircraft would probably take a ground support role in the event of war, the West would be at a great disadvantage in the initial stages of combat. Moreover, even though NATO has a greater stock of reinforcements (which, in 1976, would have increased NATO's total to 3,448 as compared with the Warsaw Pact's 3,680), it is doubtful whether such reinforcements could be fully, or speedily, utilized—particularly if airfields in the central area were destroyed in the early stages of any conflict.

Until fairly recently, NATO appeared to have the edge in terms of quality. In particular, NATO had superiority in munitions delivery accuracy, crew training and deep-strike capability. However, the Warsaw Pact had greater air defence missile capability, and a higher 'sortie rate': more flights per aircraft could be made. Furthermore, in recent years, the Pact has made great strides, particularly in electronics, and has overtaken NATO in many qualitative areas.

It is not surprising to see that West Germany and the USA are the two main NATO powers; West Germany because of its front-line position in Central Europe and the USA because of its role as a super-power. The Soviet Union is, however, by far the most powerful single country in this area. In terms of aircraft alone it has massive superiority. The reason for this is the accessibility to the Soviet Union through Central Europe.

While the quantity of Soviet tanks (at least 4.2 to NATO's every one could cause NATO alarm, NATO's superior technology partially offsets this factor. However, on balance, a traditional war (without nuclear weapons) in Central Europe would probably be fought on terms favourable to the Warsaw Pact.

Data

Ground-force manpower also includes backup personnel so leaving the number of combat troops smaller than the figures given.

Warsaw Pact figures are generally estimated and so are open to some error.

Source

Adelphi Papers, Number 127

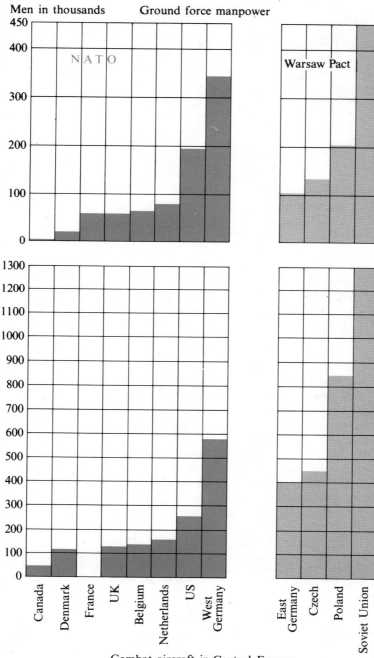

Men in thousands   Ground force manpower

NATO

Warsaw Pact

Canada
Denmark
France
UK
Belgium
Netherlands
US
West Germany

East Germany
Czech
Poland
Soviet Union

Combat aircraft in Central Europe

For the year 1976 central government and local authority receipts were as shown opposite. The difference in size of the pie charts illustrates the difference in the size of total receipts between the bodies.

The local authorities obtained most of their funds from the central government, either in the form of specific grants for items such as education or for general purposes. The specific grants, however, do not necessarily have to be used for the purpose originally intended; and this autonomy of the local authorities occasionally causes friction between central government and the local governing bodies.

In federal countries individuals pay income tax to the local authorities as well as to the central government, and these local taxes are usually the largest revenue raisers for cities and towns. Although there have occasionally been suggestions for similar plans in Britain, there has been little enthusiasm for such schemes.

The central government acquires most of its revenue through income tax, with the next largest contribution from expenditure taxes—traditionally on tobacco, alcoholic drink and petrol, as all smokers, drinkers and drivers know. However, VAT also constitutes a major component of expenditure taxes. (In the 1976/77 tax year, £3,778m was collected in VAT, while taxes raised £2,065m from hydrocarbon oils, £1,874m from tobacco, £1,138m from wines and spirits, and £807m from beer.)

The third largest source of revenue is the national insurance contributions. As has been shown, social services account for a high proportion of public authorities expenditure. While the revenue from national insurance contributions is not high enough to cover this, it goes some way to paying for the services. From this example we can see that revenue for certain items does not always finance total expenditure on those items. Conversely, car-tax was originally designed to pay for road building and maintenance. The revenue, however, exceeds the expenditure for roads, allowing these funds to be made available for other purposes. The government attempts to balance overall income and expenditure except when it wishes to spend the country out of a depression by creating a deficit or to decrease inflation by attaining a surplus.

Data

In 1976 prices central government receipts totalled £42,556m and local authority receipts £17,033m on the current account.

Source

Annual Abstract of Statistics, 1977

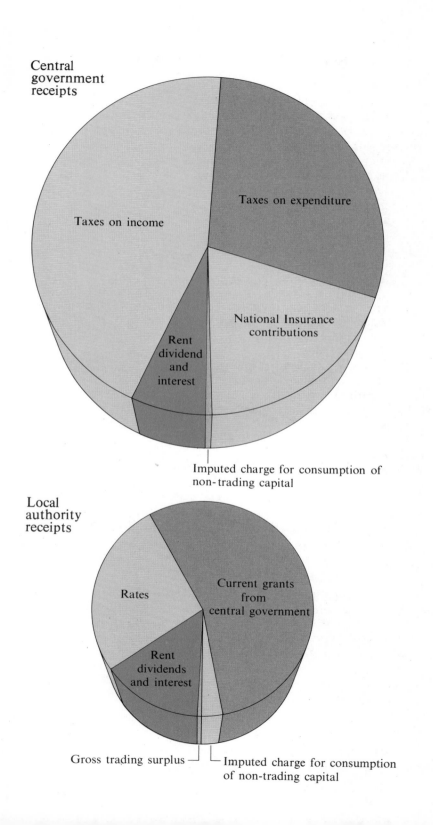

Central government receipts

Taxes on expenditure

Taxes on income

National Insurance contributions

Rent dividend and interest

Imputed charge for consumption of non-trading capital

Local authority receipts

Current grants from central government

Rates

Rent dividends and interest

Gross trading surplus

Imputed charge for consumption of non-trading capital

From the pie charts opposite it is possible to see that, by and large, the six
countries raise revenue in much the same way, although each country
attaches more importance to some categories than to others.

There are twelve such categories under which a government or local
authority may raise revenue. These are:

(1) taxes on income and wealth
(that is, taxes on personal and corporate income, death and gift
duties, etc.);
(2) social security taxes;
(3) general sales and turnover taxes;
(4) customs duties
(imports and export duties);
(5) other indirect taxes
(specific sales taxes, surplus of fiscal monopolies, taxes on foreign
exchange, taxes on property transfers, etc);
(6) other current transfers;
(7) sales and charges;
(8) surplus of government trading enterprises;
(9) interest and dividends received;
(10) sales of assets;
(11) repayments of loans granted and
(12) capital transfers.

The ways in which countries present their figures vary, because
accounting methods differ. This leads to some problems of comparison.
In the pie charts coloured shading represents as far as possible two forms
of taxes: direct taxation—taxes which are levied directly on income, etc.;
and indirect taxes—taxes which apply to expenditure, etc.

The third shade, which appears for Japan, the UK and the USA,
broadly represents social security taxes, most widespread in the three
countries mentioned.

Data

Figures for Brazil and the USA are for federal government receipts. Total
government receipts are not given because of the difficulty of adding up
each public authority's totals without double counting. Federal
government, being the largest body, has therefore been chosen.

Although the pie charts are the same size, this is not meant to imply that
all total receipts are of the same magnitude across the six countries.

The years given vary. Brazil's figures are for 1974, West Germany's for
1975, Italy's 1975, Japan's 1975, the UK's 1975, the USA's 1974.

Sources

UN Statistical Yearbooks, 1975 and 1976

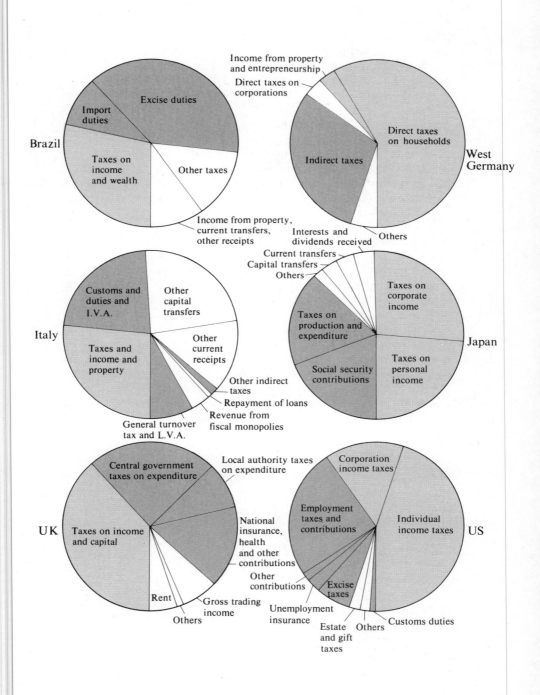

The bar charts show no overall pattern of direct taxation across the six countries. In Brazil, the UK and the USA the proportion of total receipts from direct taxation had declined, whilst in West Germany, Italy and Japan the proportion has increased.

The size of the proportion is highest in West Germany and the USA, where this form of taxation is preferred. In 1974 direct taxation accounted for roughly 60 per cent of total receipts. In Brazil and Italy less stress is placed on this tax.

Most taxation systems in operation are in progressive form: at higher levels of income a higher tax rate is charged by the government. There are, however, other possible systems. One possibility is to level the same rate on everyone no matter what their income. Another is to charge a set sum to all earners.

There are various reasons why the progressive system is used. Perhaps the main one is an attempt to maximize every individual's happiness given total wealth. The idea behind this is that a pound or a dollar, whatever monetary unit is used, is worth more to the poor than the rich. What a rich man loses in satisfaction by losing a pound is outweighed by the satisfaction a poor man gains from receiving that pound. The government acts as a means by which wealth may be redistributed.

There are, of course, arguments against this. It can be, and is, said that those individuals who receive a greater income deserve to keep it because they work harder or have special talents. The view most Western governments take is a mixture of both attitudes. They redistribute some wealth but not all so as to leave 'incentives' or 'differentials' intact. The main debate between political parties then becomes one of how much to redistribute.

Data

The figures for Brazil are taxes on income and wealth; for West Germany, income from property and entrepreneurship and direct taxes on households; for Italy, taxes on income and property; for Japan, taxes on personal and corporate income; for the UK, taxes on income and capital; for the USA, individual income tax, corporation income tax and estate and gift taxes.

Source

UN Statistical Yearbooks, 1962, 1975 and 1976

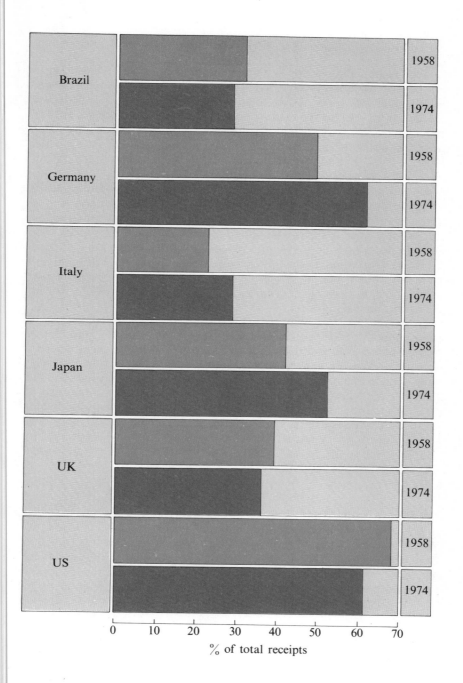

% of total receipts

A more general pattern appears when indirect taxation is analysed. In all but one of the countries—Brazil—the proportion of income received from indirect taxation has decreased. Italy has seen the most marked decline: from over 70 per cent of receipts from indirect taxation in 1958 to under 50 per cent in 1974. In the USA very little revenue has been raised by indirect taxes, with this proportion falling to an even smaller level by 1974. Even the state and local governments obtain a very low proportion of their receipts from indirect taxes.

Japan and the United States prefer to raise their revenue from sources other than expenditure tax and customs and excise. The emphasis is on letting people use their reduced incomes to buy at relatively cheap prices, rather than leaving them with a higher income which they must then allocate over goods at higher prices because of their higher tax content.

On the other hand, in the EEC countries customs duties are applied to all non-Common Market goods, forming a customs union. The criterion behind this is that by discrimination against the rest of the world, European production and wealth will be increased.

Other reasons in favour of expenditure taxes include health and environmental considerations; these apply to cigarettes and petrol particularly. It is hoped that less will be consumed as prices are raised.

In order to raise revenue, indirect taxes have to be applied in such a way as to ensure increased receipts. If taxes are too high, receipts may be reduced; and what is gained in increased revenue per item sold is lost as smaller quantities are sold. This is usually applied to those goods and services which can be defined as non-essentials or those goods which have a close substitute. A tax on butter, for example, could lead people to switch to margarine.

Data

For the USA and Brazil, federal government receipts are given.

The figures for Brazil are import duties and other indirect taxes; for West Germany, indirect taxes; for Italy, general turnover tax, revenue from fiscal monopolies, customs and excise duties and other indirect taxes; for Japan, taxes on production and expenditure; for the UK, taxes on expenditure; and for the USA, excise taxes and import duties.

Sources

UN Statistical Yearbooks, 1975 and 1976

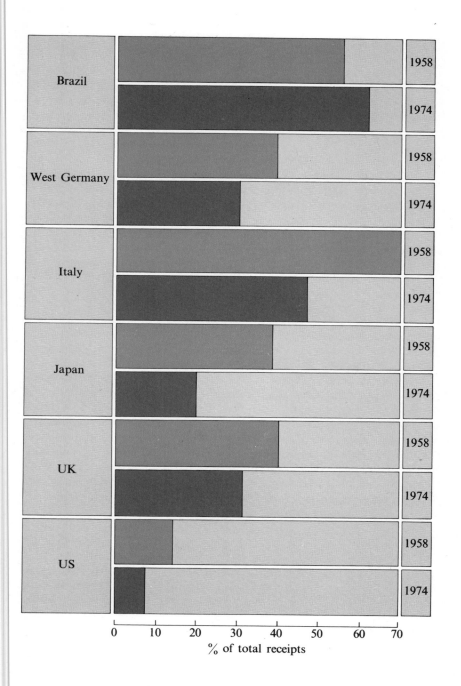

Brazil 1958 1974 West Germany 1958 1974 Italy 1958 1974 Japan 1958 1974 UK 1958 1974 US 1958 1974

0 10 20 30 40 50 60 70

% of total receipts

The top bar graph gives hours per week worked in the non-agricultural sectors (hours actually worked or hours paid for, as shown) for France, the USA, West Germany, the UK and Japan in 1956, 1966, and 1976. In the bottom graph, the percentage of the work-force in each sector is given for each country. The data is for 1975.

It can be seen that with the slight exception of France, the working week has been steadily decreasing since 1956 for the countries given. This can indicate an increase in population or, more likely in this case, an increase in the use of capital compared to labour in the economy.

The importance of the services sector in all of these economies and the small role played by agriculture is illustrated by the bottom graph. A large services sector is one of the characteristics of an advanced economy. Indeed, the size of the services sector (including transport, retailing, and wholesaling and more direct services such as dry-cleaning, haircuts and domestic help) has been called a rough measure of the 'opulence' of an economy. In the UK the distribution is: agriculture, 2.7 per cent, industry, 40.9 per cent and services, 56.4 per cent.

On the lighter side, holiday entitlements in the UK (which are normally determined by collective agreement) generally provide for at least three weeks of paid holiday a year. Non-manual workers often enjoy longer holidays than manual workers do. Annual holidays in England consist of Christmas Day and Good Friday and regular Bank holidays taking place on New Year's Day, Easter Monday, the last Monday in May, the last Monday in August and 26 December. A new bank holiday was declared on Monday, 1 May 1978 and a holiday for May Day was declared for subsequent years. Among the EEC countries, Ireland has the smallest number of public holidays (eight). The UK, the Netherlands, and Italy follow with nine public holidays each. Belgium, France, and West Germany each have ten. Luxembourg has twelve, and Denmark has thirteen public holidays. Outside the EEC, the USA has nine, Japan has twelve, and Canada has eleven public holidays.

Data

The data presented in the top graph uses 30 as a base rather than 0 to point out the differences between years. The UK data for hours of work are averages of the hours for males and females. For example, in 1976, males in the UK worked on the average 44.0 hours per week; females worked 37.4.

Sources

International Labour Office, Yearbook of Labour Statistics, 1966, 1970 and 1977
Basic Statistics of the Community, 1977

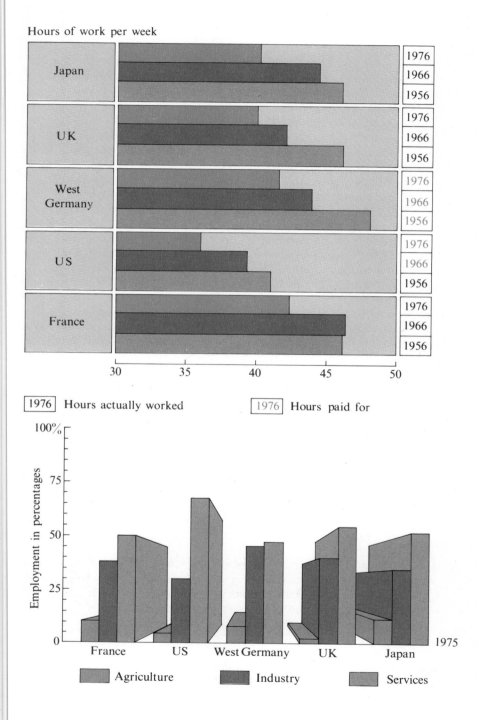

Hours of work per week

1976 Japan 1966 1956
1976 UK 1966 1956
1976 West Germany 1966 1956
1976 US 1966 1956
1976 France 1966 1956

30   35   40   45   50

1976 Hours actually worked   1976 Hours paid for

Employment in percentages

100%
75
50
25
0

France   US   West Germany   UK   Japan

1975

Agriculture   Industry   Services

The map gives investment as a percentage of Gross Domestic Product for the members of the EEC. Investment percentages for other nations are also listed. UK investment in 'real' terms (1970 prices) is shown by the graph for the years 1966 to 1976.

As can be seen, within the EEC Luxembourg uses the highest percentage of its Gross Domestic Product (29.2 per cent) for investment. At the other end of the scale, Denmark and the UK use the lowest percentage (19.9 per cent). (The average for the EEC as a whole is 21.7 per cent.) In particular, this means that in the UK, gross domestic fixed capital formation (in 1976 £9,724m, compared with £9,682m in 1971 at constant 1970 prices) represents about 20 per cent of GDP at factor cost. Within the total of gross domestic fixed capital formation in 1976, private sector investment accounted for 11.5 per cent of GDP at factor cost (12.6 per cent in 1971), general government for 4.5 per cent (5.4 per cent), and public corporations accounted for 4 per cent (3.8 per cent). Recent trends in UK investment have pointed to greater investment in North Sea oil equipment.

Comparatively low investment rates have been cited as a reason for the UK's slow economic growth. To this end, successive governments have attempted to spur investment through the use of several types of incentives, including initial allowance, investment allowances, and cash grants. These incentives have also been used with some success to boost investment in particular industries and regions. The general idea here is that investment causes growth: for example, Japan has a high growth rate and invests a lot. It does not necessarily follow, however, that there is a causal connection. Other factors such as the availability of a large supply of labour and the possibility of shifts in the labour force from one sector to another, capital and labour productivity and efficient allocation of resources, along with demand-side factors, such as the growth of exports, must be considered. Indeed, there appears to be no single, simple solution (such as investment) to the UK's relatively slow growth rate.

Data

The figures used for investment were those listed as 'gross fixed capital formation'. Gross fixed capital formation is investment in fixed assets (land, buildings, plant and machinery, vehicles and furniture) including depreciation, repairs, and maintenance expenditure.

Sources

Basic Statistics of the Community, 1977
Annual Abstract of Statistics, 1977

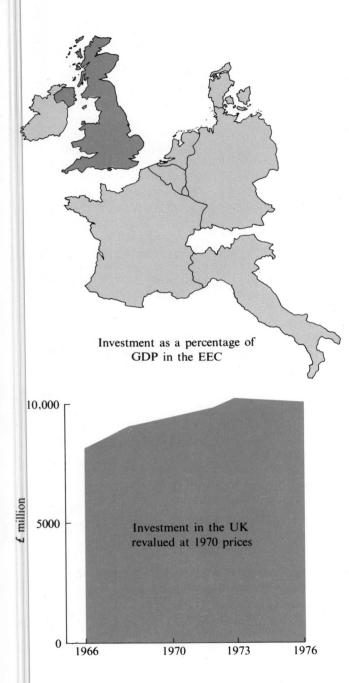

UK	19.9%
Ireland	22.3%
Denmark	19.9%
Netherlands	21.2%
West Germany	21.5%
Belgium	22.3%
Luxembourg	29.2%
France	23.4%
Italy	21.1%

Other nations:

Canada	24.1%
Japan	30.9%
Sweden	20.8%
US	16.2%

Investment as a percentage of
GDP in the EEC

£ million

10,000

5000

Investment in the UK
revalued at 1970 prices

0

1966   1970   1973   1976

Consumption of energy in the United Kingdom as measured in million therms is given by the graph for the years 1966 to 1976. The pie diagrams show the composition of energy consumption in 1976 by fuel and by consumer.

Petroleum, natural gas, coal, and nuclear power are the four main primary sources of energy consumed in the UK, along with some water power. By-products of these sources include electricity, coke, and very small quantities of town gas. About two-thirds of all primary energy used in the UK is derived from native sources, and this proportion is growing due to the abundant quantities of oil and gas discovered under the bed of the North Sea.

Petroleum was first discovered in the North Sea in 1970, and by 1977, seven fields were flowing, producing over 800,000 barrels per day of high-quality oil. This is slightly less than half the domestic requirement. Similarly, since the first natural gas was piped ashore from the North Sea in 1967, the percentage of natural gas consumed has steadily risen. Nearly all of the gas used in the UK is natural gas. Supplies of coal, the third major source of energy (and Britain's richest natural resource), were augmented in 1977 when coal deposits were discovered under the North Sea and in three mainland fields. This is expected to help extend energy self-sufficiency into the 1990s. Finally, nuclear power accounts for a sizeable proportion of electricity supplies; since 1955, a plan to expand the number of nuclear power stations has been proceeding. In 1976, inland energy consumption totalled 324.7 million tons of coal equivalent, 1.5 per cent higher than in 1975. The fuel and power industries are nationalized, except for most of the petroleum industry and part of the industry involved with the extraction of natural gas.

With the exception of the Netherlands, the UK had the smallest degree of dependence on foreign supply of energy, 43.2 per cent, in the EEC in 1975. West Germany was dependent on foreign supply for 55 per cent of its energy, France for 73.8 per cent, and Italy for 79.1 per cent.

Data

Data is listed under 'total inland energy consumption of primary fuels and equivalents', analysed by type of fuel and by class of consumer.

Source

Annual Abstract of Statistics, 1977

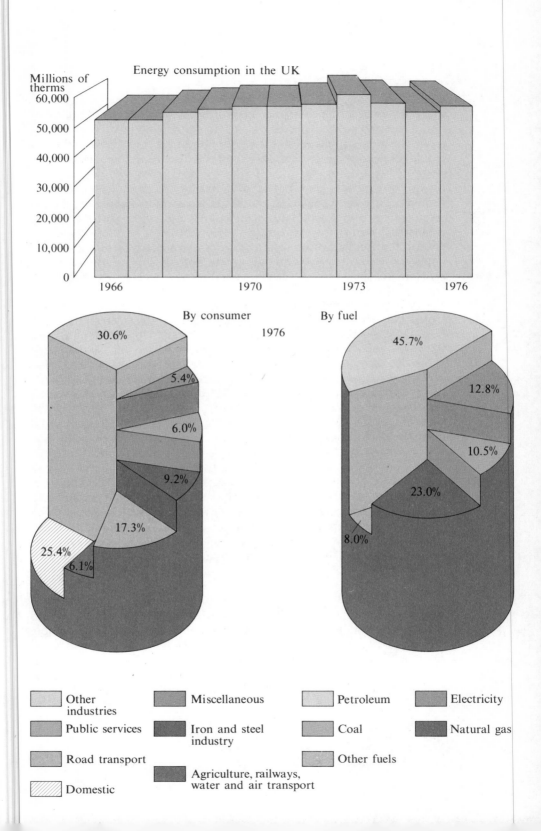

Energy consumption in the UK

Millions of therms

By consumer   1976   By fuel

Other industries	Miscellaneous
Public services	Iron and steel industry
Road transport	
Domestic	Agriculture, railways, water and air transport

Petroleum	Electricity
Coal	Natural gas
Other fuels	

The time-series graph compares the profits in real terms (1970 prices) of companies and public corporations for the years 1966 to 1976. Profits as a percentage of capital employed (1970 prices) are contrasted on the bar graph below for private companies and public corporations in the same years.

Company profits and public corporations (nationalized industry) surpluses have the same cycle, but public corporations appear to be less volatile than companies. Also significant is the steady decline of UK companies' profits as a percentage of capital employed and the slight upturn for public corporations. This is particularly worrying in its implications for private sector investment, since it is the return on earlier investments that, either directly or indirectly, largely determines the volume of future investment.

The largest public corporations include the National Coal Board, British Gas and the electricity industry, the British Steel Corporation, the Post Office, British Rail, the National Freight Corporation, British Airways, and the National Bus Company. All in all, nationalized industries account for about 10 per cent of GDP and employ 7 to 8 per cent of the national labour force. Among recent developments have been the nationalization of the shipbuilding and aircraft industries and the establishment of the British National Oil Corporation, through which the government acquired the right to buy the majority of the gas produced from the North Sea and to take measures to reduce the wastage of gas.

Public corporations are ultimately responsible to parliament. Though powers and duties are delegated to both ministers and boards (whose members are not usually civil servants), it is the boards who handle the management of the public corporations. Some of the nationalized industries receive grants from the exchequer to help with finances, while others are self-supporting. The minister of the sponsoring department generally has the power to allocate, subject to Treasury approval, any public corporation surpluses which may accrue.

Data

The profits data is found in the appropriation accounts of companies and financial institutions and public corporations, listed as 'gross trading profits' and 'gross trading surplus', respectively. Capital employed is given as 'fixed assets' in stock of fixed capital data. To be expressed in 1970 prices, actual profits and capital data is 'deflated' by multiplying the current value profits and capital data by the GDP deflator.

Sources

National Income and Expenditure, 1966–76
Economic Trends Annual Supplement

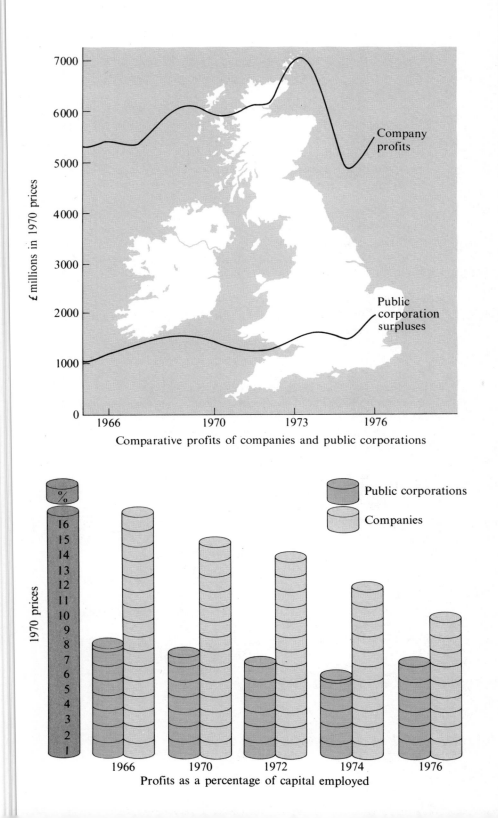

7000

6000

5000

Company profits

£ millions in 1970 prices

4000

3000

2000

Public corporation surpluses

1000

0

1966   1970   1973   1976

Comparative profits of companies and public corporations

%

Public corporations

Companies

16
15
14
13
12
11
10
9
8
7
6
5
4
3
2
1

1970 prices

1966   1970   1972   1974   1976

Profits as a percentage of capital employed

39 CAPITAL EXPENDITURES OF COMPANIES, GENERAL GOVERNMENT, AND PUBLIC CORPORATIONS

The top diagram compares the levels of capital expenditure in real terms (1970 prices) made by the private sector, general government and public corporations for the years 1962 to 1976. The pie diagrams show the distribution of employment by sector for 1971 and 1976.

The levels of investment for the private sector are clearly higher than those for general government and public corporations. (However, it is interesting to note that public corporations (nationalized companies) annually invest as much as the entire private manufacturing sector. Further, it is difficult to assess investment by general government and public corporations because social benefit as well as private profit must be considered. Indeed, nationalized industries have been seen as vehicles for a whole range of objectives such as allocation of resources, redistribution of income, dampening inflation, replacing incomes policy, and as a testing ground for industrial democracy. (Though agreement on the relative importance of these conflicting objectives has yet to be achieved!)

One view is that public enterprises should be self-financing, in order to 'reduce their claims on the nation's savings'. This, however, ignores the fact that if savings do not come from taxpayers or those who buy government bonds, consumers of the products of nationalized industries will be forced to save through higher prices.

The central government and local authorities sectors come together to form general government. Recently, there has been a shift in employment out of the private sector and into general government. In 1971, 72.9 per cent of all workers were employed in the private sector, 8.2 per cent in public corporations, with 18.9 per cent in general government. The figures in 1976, given a total employed labour force of about 24.8 million, were 70.5 per cent (17.4 million) employed in the private sector, 7.9 per cent (2 million) in public corporations, and 21.7 per cent (5.3 million) in general government. Of this 21.7 per cent, 9.5 per cent (2.3 million) was accounted for by central government and 12.2 per cent (3 million) by local authorities.

Data

The central government sector consists of all government departments, HM Forces and Women's Services and a number of other organizations, such as the National Health Service, the United Kingdom Atomic Energy Authority, and the Forestry Commission. The local authorities sector is composed of all local government authorities that have power to raise funds by means of rates or levies.

Sources

Economic Trends, December 1977
Economic Trends Annual Supplement, 1977

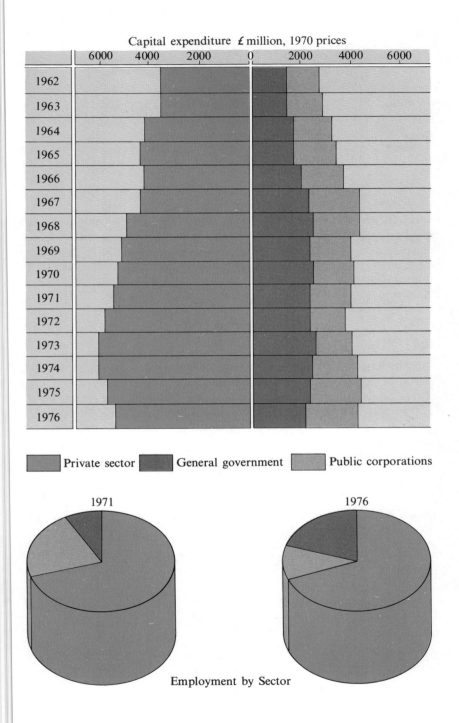

Capital expenditure £ million, 1970 prices

Private sector — General government — Public corporations

1971   1976

Employment by Sector

40 ALLOCATION OF INCOME BY NON-NATIONALIZED COMPANIES

The pie diagrams show the changing composition of income allocation by non-nationalized companies for 1956, 1966 and 1976. The area of each pie diagram is proportional to the totals of company income (expressed in 1970 prices) for each year.

Clearly, the allocation of company income has been changing, and factors such as investment incentives, incomes policy, and inflation have had a substantial impact on these changes. Taxation, for example, has steadily fallen throughout the twenty-year period, from 30 per cent of income allocation, to 17 per cent, and down to 10 per cent. Interest, on the other hand, which once took 5 per cent of income allocated in 1956, accounted for 21 per cent in 1976. The movements of dividends have been just the opposite of undistributed income after taxation (a balancing item). In 1976, just under 10 per cent of company income was allocated to dividends, while 55 per cent of the income pie was undistributed after taxation. Only the category of charity and profits due abroad has remained basically unchanged.

Data

The allocation of income data in current prices is found in the appropriation accounts of companies and financial institutions. The income totals were 'deflated' with the GDP deflator to be expressed in 1970 prices. The category of dividends includes additions to dividend reserves. The company income (to be allocated) itself is a combination of gross trading profits and rent and non-trading income plus income from abroad.

Source

Annual Abstract of Statistics, 1966 and 1977

Allocation of income by non-nationalized companies (1970 prices)

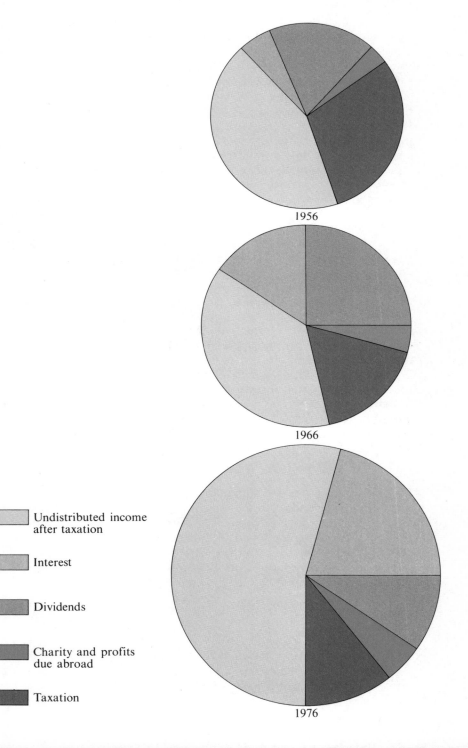

1956

1966

Undistributed income
after taxation

Interest

Dividends

Charity and profits
due abroad

Taxation

1976

Labour productivity (often referred to simply as 'productivity') is crudely measured by the ratio of output to the number of persons employed. Thus, productivity increases correspond to increases in output per person employed.

The time-series graph at the top of the page opposite shows how productivity has changed in five countries over the period 1967 to 1976. It should be noted that the productivity series for each country is based on 1970 = 100; this means that the graph can show changes only in *relative* productivity—absolute differences can not be inferred from this presentation. The most striking feature of this graph is the strong increase in Japanese productivity: over this period, output per person increased at an average rate of almost 9 per cent per year. It is also interesting to note that, although the UK comes fairly low down the 'growth table', the 'wooden spoon' is taken by the US, with productivity increasing at just 2.1 per cent per year.

International comparisons of the *absolute* differences in labour productivity are notoriously difficult to make; a large number of factors limit the usefulness of inferences drawn from such comparisons. However, some crude indication is provided by the table at the foot of the page. This shows that output per person (within manufacturing industry) in the United States was well over double that in the United Kingdom in 1971, whereas West Germany and France both recorded productivity levels over 50 per cent higher than in the UK. Some of these marked differences can clearly be accounted for by the fact that workers in the UK have less (and less efficient) machinery to work with than their foreign counterparts; nevertheless, this is only a partial explanation. (Indeed, there are strong arguments suggesting that some machinery is not used to its full efficiency because of overmanning and various restrictive practices.)

Data

Slight differences in the definitions of productivity exist. For West Germany, Japan and the UK, the output series is that of net production; for the US, it is gross production. The output series is expressed relative to the number of employed persons for all countries except Japan; for this country, the number of man-days is used instead.

The table is reproduced from Pratten's study (see below), to which further reference could be made for more details.

Sources

Yearbook of Labour Statistics, 1977
Pratten, C. F., *Labour Productivity Differentials within International Companies*, University of Cambridge, Department of Applied Economics, Occasional Papers 50

Indices (1970=100) of labour productivity in manufacturing industry

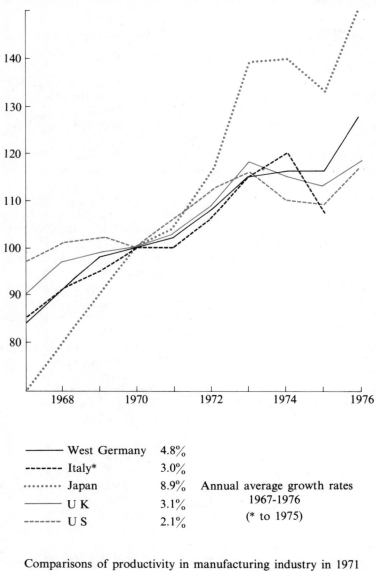

	West Germany	4.8%	
-------	Italy*	3.0%	
········	Japan	8.9%	Annual average growth rates
———	U K	3.1%	1967-1976
-------	U S	2.1%	(* to 1975)

Comparisons of productivity in manufacturing industry in 1971

	UK	US	West Germany	France
Index (UK=100)	100	216	159	155
Productivity differential with UK in 1971	-	+116%	+59%	+55%

Corporation tax as a percentage of total tax revenue in 1970 is given for various countries by the bar graph. At the bottom, rates of corporation tax are listed. The rates are for 1974.

Corporation tax is levied on taxable company profits, whether distributed or not. Since 1973, an 'imputations' system has been in effect in the UK. According to this system, two items are deducted from gross profits to arrive at taxable profits: the depreciation allowance set by the Inland Revenue and the interest charges on the company's financial obligations. After these deductions, the profits are taxed. Since 1974, the corporation tax has been 52 per cent with a reduced rate of 42 per cent for small companies (as defined in the Finance Acts 1972, 1974 and 1977). The post-tax profits are then split between retained earnings and dividends to the shareholders. Though income tax is not deducted from dividends, a company must make an advance payment of corporation tax to the Inland Revenue if it distributes profits to its shareholders.

Recently, the corporation tax has yielded on average around £2,500m per year. The figure is quite variable, due to the volatility of profits, companies' freedom in the timing of depreciation allowances, and simply, the changing of rates. Comparisons between nations of levels of tax are always difficult since fiscal systems differ. Compared to equivalent rates outside the UK, however, British rates of corporate taxation were somewhat higher—the situation has changed slightly with the reform of 1975, which deferred tax due on profits attributable to stock appreciation (an increase in value). As to who finally pays corporation tax (incidence), this depends crucially on the market environment: sometimes it is the companies who suffer a reduction in post-tax incomes, but in other cases, it is the consumer who pays in the form of higher prices.

Data

The percentages of corporation tax are listed under a breakdown of revenue from taxation as *direct* taxes. The rates given of corporate taxation are those of the basic corporation tax.

It is important to note that the percentage of corporation tax in total tax revenues depends on three things: (1) the rate at which tax is levied on corporations; (2) the taxable income of corporations (these two determining the absolute corporate tax bill); and (3) the absolute magnitude of receipts from other forms of taxation. Thus, for example, a low corporation tax percentage could indicate either (1) a low *rate* of tax; or (2) a low taxable income; or (3) high taxation elsewhere (or a combination of all three).

Sources

Basic Statistics of the Community
European Marketing Data and Statistics 1975/76

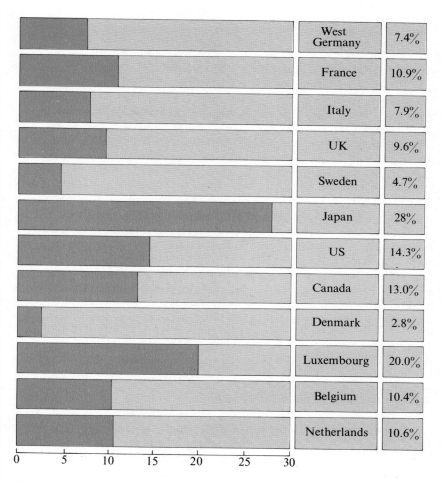

Percentage of corporation tax in total tax revenue

Rates of corporate taxation:

France	50	US	48
UK	42/52	Japan	40
Netherlands	45-48	Italy	18-25
West Germany	56	Belgium	42

43 UNEMPLOYMENT

The graph shows the unemployment rates of a selection of countries. The countries shown have had widely differing unemployment experiences over the period. Unemployment in Italy during the 1950s and early 1960s fell from a very high level to one more moderate by international standards. The 1950s also saw a marked decline in unemployment in West Germany from over 7 per cent to under 1 per cent, and a very low level of unemployment was maintained in Germany until 1973. This year marked a significant increase in a number of countries. Japan has experienced consistently low unemployment throughout the period although the period since 1973 shows a significant increase by Japan's own historical standards. The USA has experienced rather high unemployment, by comparison with other countries over the whole period. UK unemployment has been moderate by international standards but the 1977 level is the highest since the war. Although unemployment rates may be determined largely by characteristics specific to the country concerned, the international climate may sometimes play a significant role. For instance, the period since 1973 has been characterized by a general increase in the level of unemployment. Worldwide influences include, for instance, the substantial increases in oil prices.

Data

Unemployment statistics from different countries are not really comparable, because of differences in definition of the unemployed and in data collection methods. In most European countries unemployment is measured either by numbers of insured workers claiming benefit or by numbers registered with the state employment service. In the USA and Japan data is collected by sample survey. Divergences between actual numbers of people looking for work and registered unemployment occurs, for example, in the UK through married women not paying the full National Insurance being ineligible for unemployment benefit. This lack of financial inducement reduces the level of registration of the unemployed. Insofar as financial inducements to register vary over countries or over time, then the data must be interpreted with this in mind. Work has been done by the Bureau of Labour Statistics in Washington to present international data in comparable form; their estimates are shown in the table.

Sources

UN Statistical Yearbook
International Labour Office, Bulletin of Labour Statistics

Unemployment rates of selected countries

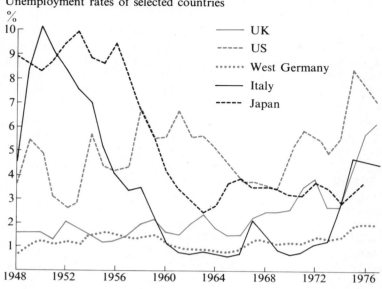

International unemployment rates:
   as published and adjusted to US concepts

		1970	1971	1972	1973	1974	1975
Great Britain	as published	2.5	3.4	3.7	2.6	2.6	4.1
	adjusted	3.0	3.8	4.2	2.9	2.9	4.9
Italy	as published	3.2	3.2	3.7	3.5	2.9	3.3
	adjusted	3.5	3.5	4.0	3.8	3.1	3.6
Japan	as published	1.2	1.2	1.4	1.3	1.4	1.9
	adjusted	1.2	1.3	1.4	1.3	1.4	1.9
West Germany	as published	0.7	0.8	1.1	1.2	2.6	4.8
	adjusted	0.5	0.7	0.9	1.0	2.1	3.9

Unemployment statistics are only one side of the labour market; they provide an indication of the outstanding demand for jobs. The other side of the coin is, of course, the demand for workers. Firms with outstanding vacancies may try to fill them by registering them with local employment offices. Some vacancies are not registered, but are filled by, for example, newspaper advertisements.

Registered unemployment and vacancy statistics are plotted in the diagrams opposite. In the upper graph both employment and vacancies are plotted against time.

The unemployment data has been characterized by cycles of about five years, showing a moderate upward trend to the late 1960s. The 1970s have seen a steep upturn in this trend with unemployment much higher than the post-war average. Registered vacancies have moved in a cycle, as would be expected, in the opposite direction to unemployment. There is a clear negative relation between the two series.

The second graph illustrates a supposed change in the relationship between employment and vacancies. A Department of Employment (DoE) working party decided that the shift in the relationship between unemployment and vacancies was equivalent to about 300,000 jobs in the level of unemployment corresponding to a given level of vacancies (that is, the vacancies–unemployment 'relationship' shifted rightwards by some 300,000). There is a variety of possible explanations. The introduction in December 1966 of an earnings related supplement to national insurance benefits increased the financial incentive to register when unemployed. The DoE working party concluded that legislative changes could not account for more than about 70,000 jobs. Another possible explanation is that firms may find that registration of vacancies is a relatively more efficient way of finding workers when employment exchanges have a large number of workers on their books.

Data

Statistics relate to the wholly unemployed and to vacancies registered with employment exchanges.

Sources

British Labour Statistics Historical Abstract, tables 165 and 179
Department of Employment Gazettes

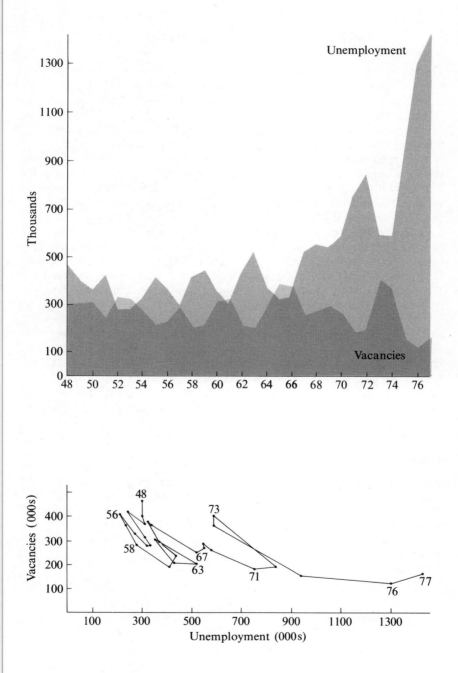

The incidence of unemployment is by no means evenly spread across the regions of the United Kingdom. Shown in the diagram are the average unemployment rates for the United Kingdom standard regions for the two periods 1949–64 and 1965–75.

Northern Ireland has faced by far the worst unemployment figures, followed by Scotland, Wales and the north of England. The high unemployment in these regions may be explained at least partly by their having a large proportion of the declining and slowly growing industries. The shipbuilding industry is largely concentrated in Northern Ireland, Scotland and the north. Coal mining is predominantly located in Wales, Scotland and the north.

It is a matter of government policy to reduce the differences in unemployment rates between regions. Regional policy includes investment grants, the control of Industrial Development Certificates (IDCs) and, after 1968, the introduction of a Regional Employment Premium (REP) whereby employers are subsidized in their employment of labour in development areas.

The pie charts display the number of employees (employed and unemployed) by region in 1951 and in 1975. The major changes over this period are the increase in the proportion of the labour force located in the south-west from 5.3 per cent to 6.7 per cent and the decrease in the figures for the north-west from 13.9 per cent to 11.9 per cent. The proportion of the labour force in Northern Ireland, despite the chronically high unemployment and other troubles, has if anything increased.

Data

The data refers to the UK standard regions. For the period up to 1965 combined data only is available for Yorkshire and Humberside and the East Midlands and for the south-east and East Anglia. Unemployment rates refer to the wholly unemployed.

Sources

British Labour Statistics Historical Abstract, tables 168 and 131.
   (Appendix E provides a definition of the standard regions.)
British Labour Statistics Yearbooks (for data after 1968)

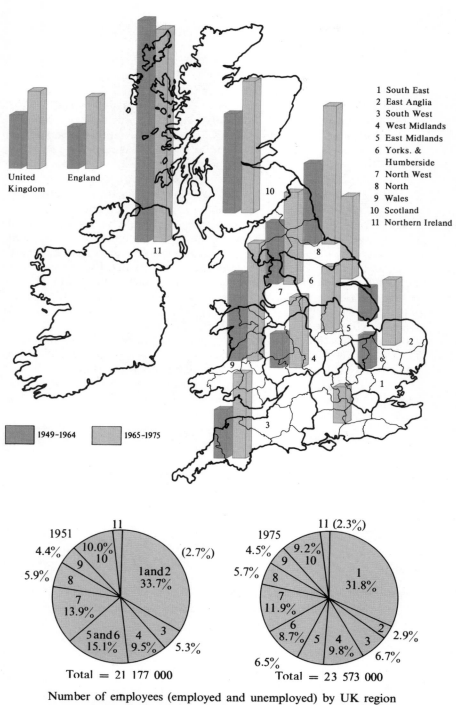

United Kingdom

England

1 South East
2 East Anglia
3 South West
4 West Midlands
5 East Midlands
6 Yorks. & Humberside
7 North West
8 North
9 Wales
10 Scotland
11 Northern Ireland

1949-1964   1965-1975

1951

11
10.0% 10
4.4% 9
5.9% 8
7 13.9%
5 and 6 15.1%
4 9.5%
3 5.3%
1 and 2 33.7%
(2.7%)

Total = 21 177 000

1975

11 (2.3%)
9.2% 10
4.5% 9
5.7% 8
7 11.9%
6 8.7%
5 6.5%
4 9.8%
3 6.7%
2 2.9%
1 31.8%

Total = 23 573 000

Number of employees (employed and unemployed) by UK region
1 South East 2 E Anglia 3 S West 4 W Midlands 5 E Midlands
6 Yorkshire & Humberside 7 North West 8 North 9 Wales
10 Scotland 11 Northern Ireland

The diagrams show the changing structure of employment in the British economy. The top two pie charts show the number of employees employed in a selection of industries in 1959 and 1977. Clearly, the primary and staple industries have been declining whilst the service sector of the economy has been expanding. Miscellaneous services include: betting and gambling; hotels and other residential establishments; public houses and clubs; motor repairers, garages and filling stations; and other services. Professional and scientific services include, among others: educational services (which have grown particularly rapidly, from 881,000 in 1959 to 1,620,000 in 1973); legal services; medical and dental services; and research and development services. The vehicles section is composed not only of motor vehicle manufacture, which has expanded in employment over the period, but also aerospace equipment manufacturing and railway carriage manufacture, which have declined. The observed shift in employment may be explained by, for instance, increased foreign competition reducing Britain's share in world markets. On the other hand, modern techniques of production may require less but better educated labour.

The second two pie charts show the proportion of workers by occupation; as might be expected, the trend is away from manual work. The shift in the occupational distribution of the labour force might simply reflect the shift from industries with a high proportion of manual labour to those with a small proportion; for instance, from mining to educational services. On the other hand, there may be, in addition, shifts in the occupational structure within industries.

Data

The industry groups relate to the 1968 Standard Industrial Classification. The DoE has calculated continuous employment estimates back to 1959 in order to eliminate a number of discontinuities otherwise occurring in the data. Occupational statistics are taken from a special article in the October 1975 Gazette.

Sources

Department of Employment Gazettes, March 1975, October 1975 and later issues

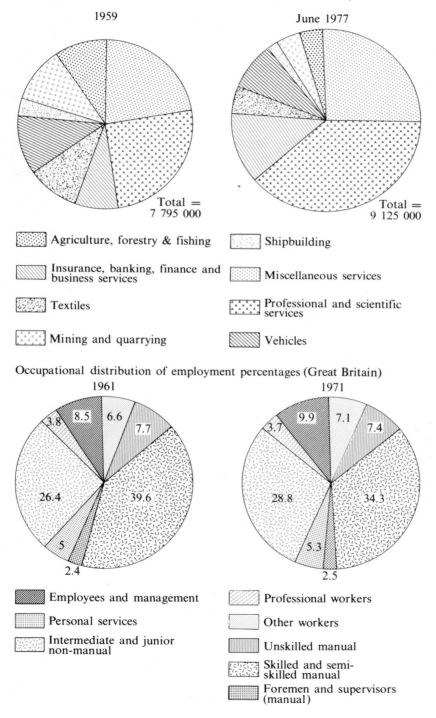

Employees in employment in selected industries (Great Britain)

1959

June 1977

Total =
7 795 000

Total =
9 125 000

Agriculture, forestry & fishing

Shipbuilding

Insurance, banking, finance and business services

Miscellaneous services

Textiles

Professional and scientific services

Mining and quarrying

Vehicles

Occupational distribution of employment percentages (Great Britain)

1961

1971

Employees and management

Professional workers

Personal services

Other workers

Intermediate and junior non-manual

Unskilled manual

Skilled and semi-skilled manual

Foremen and supervisors (manual)

The upper diagram shows the percentage of registered unemployed by duration of unemployment. At any time the registered unemployed constitute a stock into which flow new entrants and from which flow those finding jobs. Each month the flows on and off the register are of the order of 300,000 jobs—about 4 million per year. So relatively small increases in flows onto the register or decreases in the flows off it can make a significant difference to the unemployment rate at the end of the year. When unemployment is increasing there is a relatively large number of new entrants to the register; these new entrants reduce the proportion of long-term unemployed. As the level of unemployment begins to decrease, recent entrants to the register are often most easily placed, and the proportion of long-term unemployed increases. From the diagram it can be seen that the proportion unemployed for more than any specified length of time moves cyclically. The lower diagram shows the increase in average annual unemployment on the net flow onto the register. The peaks of the long-term (over 52 weeks) unemployed coincide with the troughs in the net flow onto the register.

The proportion of long-term unemployed may vary not only with the rate of inflow and outflow from the register, but also with the level of unemployment. Other factors may also have an influence: for example, whether or not employers regard those out of work for long periods as lazy; or perhaps workers become discouraged after a certain time and no longer actively look for work; either of these factors would influence the proportion of long-term unemployed. The upper diagram shows that the proportion of workers unemployed for longer periods has increased. In January 1978 nearly 80 per cent of those unemployed had been so for over eight weeks; the average for the 1950s was about 50 per cent.

Data

The figures have been calculated from quarterly data. The 1978 figure relates to January of that year only. Data up to March 1962 was collected at March, June, September and December; from this date at January, April, July and October.

Sources

British Labour Statistics Historical Abstract, table 175
British Labour Statistics Yearbooks
Department of Employment Gazettes

Registered unemployment by duration of unemployment

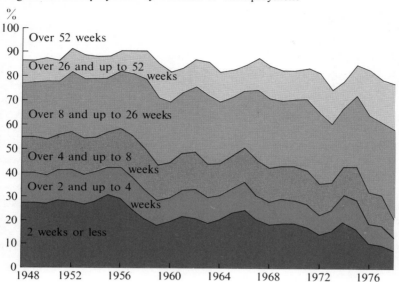

Changes in unemployment (000s)

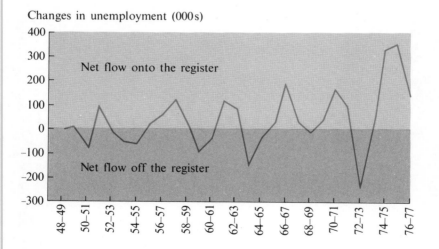

By 1920, the membership of trade unions had risen to over four times its turn of the century level. 1921 saw a substantial drop in membership, which may have resulted from the very large increase in unemployment in that year—from about 4 per cent in 1920 to 17 per cent in 1921. Membership continued to decline until the mid-1930s, after which it has increased, its present level being the highest ever. Male membership now increases rather slowly, in contrast to the rapid rise in female membership. Female membership also grew quickly during the two world wars, reflecting the increased female participation in the labour force.

Between 1890 and 1920 the number of trade unions varied between 1,200 and 1,300. Since 1920, however, the number has decreased steadily, even in a period of rapidly growing membership. Unions have been growing and forming large amalgamated unions. In 1938 nearly 17 per cent of unionized labour formed unions of fewer than 10,000 members; 49 per cent were in unions of over 100,000 members. The trend from small to large unions gives advantages to union members of, for instance, the possibility of national wage negotiations.

Data

The statistics relate to all organizations of employees with head offices in the United Kingdom that are known to include among their objectives negotiating with employers with a view to regulating the terms and conditions of employment of their members. This includes organizations of salaried and professional workers as well as manual wage earners. Both registered and unregistered trade unions are included in this definition.

Sources

British Labour Statistics Historical Abstract, table 196
British Labour Statistics Yearbooks (for figures after 1968)

Membership of trade unions at five-year intervals (1900-1975)

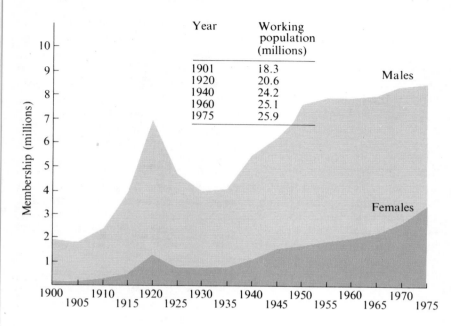

Year	Working population (millions)
1901	18.3
1920	20.6
1940	24.2
1960	25.1
1975	25.9

Number of trade unions at five-year intervals (1900-1975)

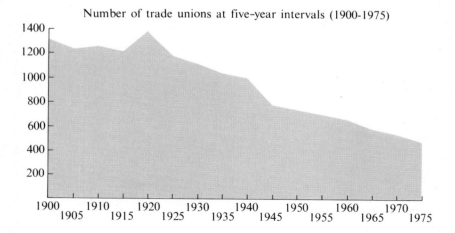

The figures relate to unions voluntarily registered under the trade union acts of 1871 and 1913. In 1947 there were 417 such organizations; by 1970 the number had fallen to 326. Membership in registered unions had risen over this same period from 7,758,000 to 9,277,000. At the end of 1947 registered trade unions held funds totalling £50,081,000; at the end of 1970 the figure was £134,599,000.

By far the largest source of trade union income is membership subscriptions; other sources of income include rent on premises and income from investments. Working expenses constitute the largest component of expenditure and have risen as a proportion of total expenditure over the period since 1947. Unemployment and dispute expenses fluctuate, as would be expected, with strike activity in the economy. They constitute in an average year a rather small proportion of total expenses. Provident benefits include expenditure on sickness and accident benefit, death benefit and superannuation. Provident benefits have fallen from 29 per cent of total expenditure in 1947 to 21 per cent in 1970. Other expenses include the political fund.

Data

In 1971 the Conservative government introduced a new Industrial Relations Act that was opposed by parts of the trade union movement. Two-hundred and twenty-nine organizations registered under the new act but they had a combined membership of only 891,000 members. As a result, no comparable figures on trade union funds are available after this date.

Source

Annual Abstract of Statistics

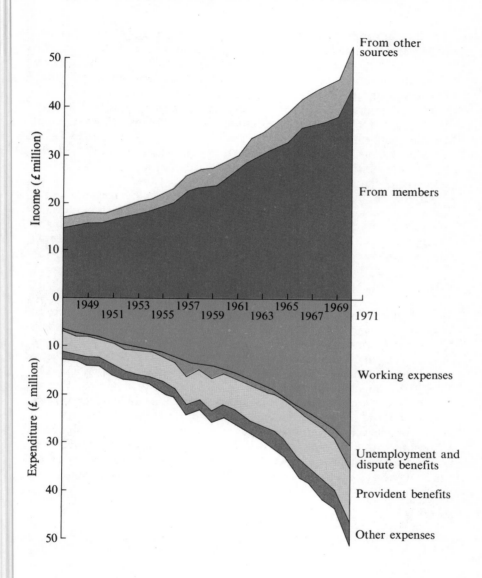

Income and expenditure of registered trade unions in Great Britain

50 WORKING DAYS LOST THROUGH INDUSTRIAL DISPUTES

The diagram opposite charts the five-year moving average of the number of days lost through industrial disputes per thousand persons employed in a selection of countries. The United Kingdom record has been fairly moderate by international standards, although since the late 1960s there has been a sharp upward trend in the average.

Most nations seem to lose more work days now than at the beginning of this period. Of the nineteen countries for which the Department of Employment publishes data, only the USA averaged more than 1,000 days lost for the period 1953–64. But between 1966 and 1975, Australia (1,036 days lost), Canada (1,849), India (1,379) and Italy (1,766) in addition to the USA (1,337) all lost more than 1,000 days.

Of the countries shown in the diagram, Germany has enjoyed a relatively small number of days lost. Other countries with favourable records are Sweden (49 days lost for 1966–75), Norway (61) and the Netherlands (62). At the extreme is Switzerland, which has averaged only one working day lost per 1,000 employees over the ten years 1966–75.

Data

The definitions used in the gathering of statistics vary from country to country, so they are not strictly comparable. In the UK, stoppages involving fewer than ten workers and those lasting less than one day are excluded from the figures except where the aggregate number of days lost exceeds one hundred. Stoppages include both strikes and lockouts. The UK figures include workers directly and indirectly involved; that is, workers who, although not themselves a party to the dispute, are thrown out of work at the establishment concerned. The figures exclude loss of time; for example, through shortages of material at other establishments. The international figures are based on a selection of industries only, comprising mining, manufacturing, construction and transport. In the case of the USA, electricity and sanitary services are also included.

Sources

Department of Employment Gazettes

International comparison of days lost through industrial disputes

(5 - year averages)

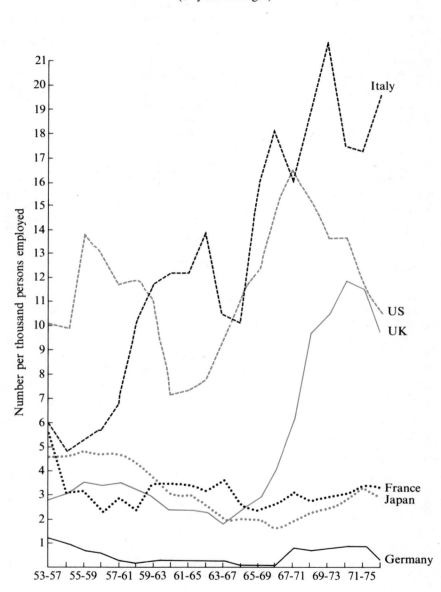

The relatively large number of days lost through industrial disputes at the end of the last century was followed by a comparatively trouble-free beginning to the twentieth century. The year 1908 saw over 10 million days lost for the first time in the century, and this signalled the beginning of a period, costly in terms of days lost, which lasted until the outbreak of the First World War. The coal mining industry alone lost more than 30 million days in 1912. The First World War was a period of relative quiescence, but this was followed by an immediate upsurge in strike activity. The period after the war was a time of very high unemployment in the UK; international circumstances had left the pound overvalued and government policy favoured a general cut in wages and prices rather than devaluation. Attempted wage cuts led to confrontations with the labour force, especially with the miners, which culminated in the General Strike of 1926. Over 162 million working days were lost in that year, over 146 million in coal mining alone—considerably more than the entire economy lost over the next 20 years.

The period since 1970 has been characterized by large numbers of working days lost relative to the period since the General Strike. The number of days lost in 1972 was the highest since 1926, with stoppages on a national scale by coalminers, building operatives and dockworkers accounting for nearly two-thirds of this total. A substantial part of strike activity in the 1970s has been due to pay claims in excess of government prescribed limits.

The number of strikes per year has risen over the period. The number in coal mining increased up to the mid 1950s, when by far the largest proportion of stoppages beginning in any year belonged to this industry. The decline in the number of strikes in coal mining since this time has been matched by an increased number in the rest of the economy.

Data

The statistics refer to the number of stoppages beginning in any year; number of working days lost refer to stoppages in progress in the particular year. Stoppages that involve fewer than ten workers or lasted less then one day are not included, unless the aggregate number of days lost exceeded 100. See also the discussion under topic 50.

Sources

British Labour Statistics Historical Abstract, table 197
British Labour Statistics Yearbooks

Aggregate number of working days lost in UK in stoppages in progress in year
(millions)

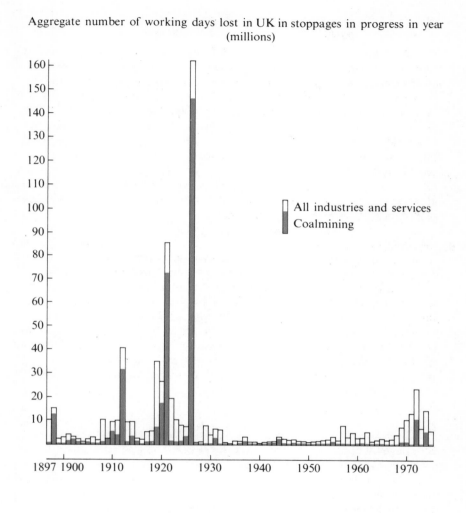

All industries and services
Coalmining

Number of stoppages in UK beginning in year

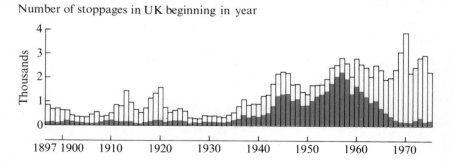

The incidence of industrial disputes is not evenly spread across the economy. Shown opposite are data for the ten industries that lost the most working days per 1,000 employees because of stoppages during the period 1966–73. In some industries a single dispute makes a significant or even major contribution to the eight-year average. In coal mining, for example, the number of working days lost in a year varies from 181 per 1,000 workers in 1971 to 32,732 in 1972. In postal services and telecommunications 14,086 days were lost in 1971, a single strike which constituted by far the greater part of days lost over the whole period. Other industries experienced moderately large numbers of days lost in almost every year; port and inland water transport and the motor vehicle manufacturing industry are in this category.

The high variation in industrial disputes across the economy is highlighted by the fact that in a typical year almost 98 per cent of manufacturing establishments are free of industrial stoppages. These constitute about 80 per cent of the total employment in manufacturing.

Recently there has been interest in the relationship between size of manufacturing plant and incidence of industrial stoppages. From the table it can be seen that the larger the plant, the more likely it is to be affected by disputes. Larger plants, on average, lose more working days per 1,000 employees than do smaller plants. This may be explained by closer working relationships between managers and workers in smaller plants or by the fact that larger plants are concentrated in the highly stoppage-affected industries.

Data

Stoppages include both strikes and lockouts. The statistics relate to all workers thrown out of work at the establishment concerned—even where they are not themselves a party to the dispute. Consequently the figures do not really measure 'strike-proneness'. The industries named are from the 1968 Standard Industrial Classification (SIC) and relate to minimum list headings.

Sources

Department of Employment Gazettes, February 1976 and January 1978

The ten most stoppage-affected industries in the UK (by working days lost per 1000 employees average 1966-73)

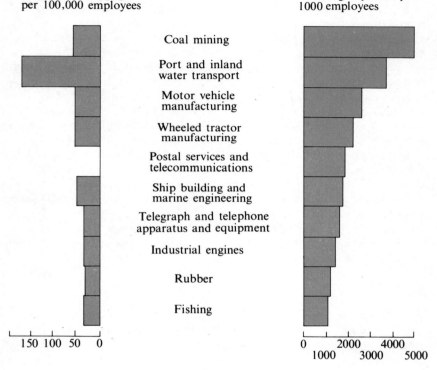

Number of stoppages per 100,000 employees

Working days lost per 1000 employees

Coal mining

Port and inland water transport

Motor vehicle manufacturing

Wheeled tractor manufacturing

Postal services and telecommunications

Ship building and marine engineering

Telegraph and telephone apparatus and equipment

Industrial engines

Rubber

Fishing

150 100 50 0

0   2000   4000
1000   3000   5000

Incidence of stoppages by plant size (GB manufacturing)

Number of establishments	% of total employment in establishments unaffected by stoppages (average 1971-75)	Number of working days lost per 1000 employees (average 1971-73)
11-99	99.3	43.6
100-199	96.8	155.0
200-499	93.0	329.1
500-999	83.4	719.4
1000 or more	51.1	2046.1
Total	79.5	

The financial surplus/deficit of a domestic sector represents the sum available for the net acquisition of financial claims on other domestic sectors or for net investment in real or in financial investments abroad. Shown in the diagram are the financial surpluses from 1952 for three domestic sectors: the public, the private and the sector of industrial and commercial companies. The public sector comprises central government, local authorities and public corporations. The sector of industrial and commercial companies refers to private firms resident in the United Kingdom. The personal sector consists of individuals, unincorporated businesses, agricultural companies and charities and private trusts.

A financial surplus for the overseas sector is the counterpart of a deficit on current account in the UK balance of payments, and equals net overseas investment in the UK. An overseas sector deficit represents a UK current account surplus on UK investment abroad.

The diagram shows that the public sector has been in financial deficit for the entire period between 1952 and 1976, with the exception of 1969 and 1970. Up to 1960 this deficit was largely counterbalanced by a financial surplus in the industrial and commercial companies sector. Since 1960 a large personal sector surplus has balanced the public sector deficit. The marked increase in the size of all the figures after 1970 can, of course, partly be accounted for by inflation but also indicate considerable real increases.

Data

Figures for the years 1952–63 are taken from estimates made in 1967, which may not be as accurate for those of the later period but should display the trends well enough. Data is also available for the banking sector and other financial institutions but is not represented here. Figures for all sectors should add up to zero, but in practice they do not as figures for income and expenditure are calculated separately.

Sources

Bank of England Quarterly Bulletin, December 1967
Bank of England Statistical Abstract, No. 2
Financial Statistics

Net acquisition of financial assets: various sectors

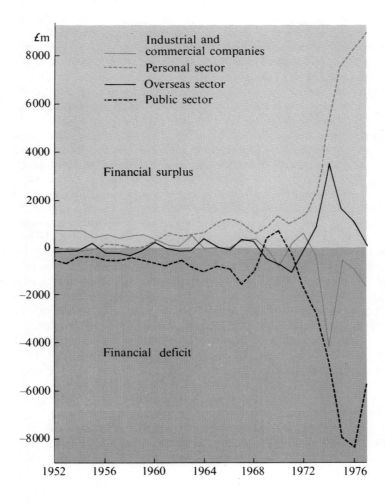

Domestic credit expansion (DCE) can be defined as the public sector borrowing requirement (PSBR) minus purchases of public sector debt by the non-bank private sector plus the increase in bank lending in sterling to the private sector and to the overseas sector. This definition is revised from that used in the UK from 1969 to December 1976; lending to the UK private sector in foreign currencies for direct and portfolio investment was excluded in 1976 because it had no appreciable effect on domestic liquidity. DCE has been recalculated on the new definition back to the second quarter of 1971. The diagram shows DCE and its components on the new definition from this date; the figures given for DCE for earlier years relate to the old definition and are given for comparison.

The public sector borrowing requirement indicates the extent to which the public sector borrows from other domestic sectors and overseas to finance the balance of receipts arising from its various activities. It is financed in three main ways; by sales of debt to the public, by borrowing from banks and by transactions with residents of other countries.

The diagram shows that the PSBR increased from financial year 1971–72, reaching a peak in 1975–76. An increase in the net acquisition of public debt by the non-bank private sector and a decrease in bank lending in sterling from 1973 to 1974 more than compensate for the rise in PSBR. As a result, DCE reaches a peak in 1973–74. Since that time DCE has decreased by some £2,500m. Even bearing in mind the differences in definition, it is clear that the period 1969–70 to 1973–74 represents a very substantial increase in DCE by historical standards.

Data

The flow of DCE was previously defined as: the change in domestic non-bank holdings of notes and coins, plus lending to the public sector by UK banks and from overseas, plus lending by UK banks in sterling and foreign currencies to the private sector (other than lending in foreign currencies for investment overseas), plus lending by UK banks in sterling to the overseas sector.

Sources

Bank of England Statistical Abstract, No. 2
Financial Statistics

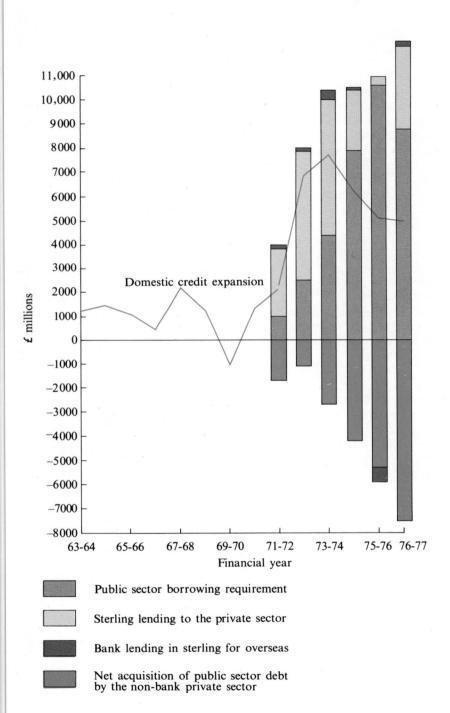

£ millions

Domestic credit expansion

Financial year

Public sector borrowing requirement

Sterling lending to the private sector

Bank lending in sterling for overseas

Net acquisition of public sector debt
by the non-bank private sector

The graph opposite plots a selection of interest rates and the dividend yield derived from the *Financial Times* index of industrial ordinary shares (base 1 July 1973 = 100). The Bank of England minimum lending rate (which used to be known as Bank Rate) is the rate at which the central bank acting as a lender of the last resort normally lends to members of the discount market against securities of treasury bills. This rate strongly influences other interest rates in the economy. It can be seen from the diagram that the rates on the London clearing banks deposit accounts follows the path of the minimum lending rate (MLR) very closely but at a lower level. The Building Society Association recommended rate follows the trend but fluctuates much less than the rate on deposit accounts. The dividend yield on shares is not so directly influenced by the MLR and does not follow it in such a simple manner.

Interest rates have a number of roles in the economy. High interest rates make borrowing expensive, for consumer expenditure on, for instance, cars and houses, and for firms borrowing for investment purposes. Interest rates influence the amount of public debt the private sector is willing to hold and a high level of interest rates may attract foreign speculative or 'hot' money into the United Kingdom.

Data

Statistics refer to the end-of-year rates except for the *Financial Times* index of industrial ordinary shares dividend yield for which the figures relate to the average of working days. Building society rates are given net of income tax where this is paid by societies at the agreed composite rates. The deposit account rate is for 7 days notice and on deposits of less than £10,000. From 13 October 1972, the minimum lending rate will normally be $\frac{1}{2}$ per cent higher than the average rate of discount for treasury bills established at the weekly tender, rounded to the nearest $\frac{1}{4}$ per cent above. The central bank may suspend the operation of this rule, however, if other circumstances make it inappropriate.

Source

Economic Trends Annual Supplement, 1977, Table 151

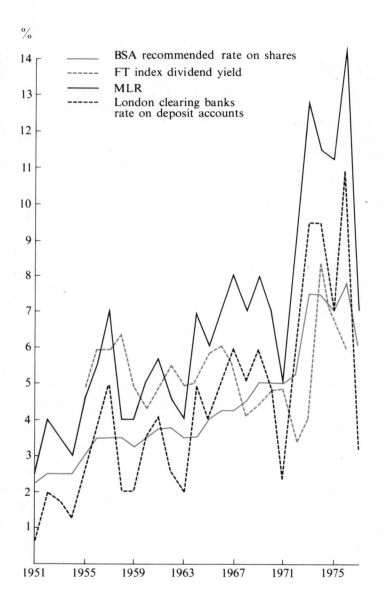

%

14 ── BSA recommended rate on shares
----- FT index dividend yield
13 ─── MLR
----- London clearing banks
12   rate on deposit accounts

The first estimate of population was made for England and Wales in 1086 from the number of families in the Domesday Book. The first full census was taken in 1801, with returns being made by such persons as vicars or school masters on behalf of the parish or district. Today census returns are made by each household. The bar graphs presented here illustrate the growth of the UK population and its distribution by age and sex for the period 1871–1976.

The ratio of females to males in the population has been fairly constant. From about 1.06 in the period up to 1911, the proportion rose to over 1.08 in 1931 and 1951, then declined to 1.05 in 1976. However, except in 1901, there have been more males than females in the 0–19 age group. This balance of the sexes is reversed in all other age groups up to 1951, but is maintained through the 20–40 age range before switching in the 1961–76 period. This suggests that the ladies have shown greater staying power, but that the trend may be changing.

The age distribution shows its main changes in the 0–19 and over 60 age groups. The proportion of the population in the former was declining slowly up to 1911 but then fell sharply following the First World War as is shown in the 1931 column, and fell further after the Second World War. From 1951 there is an upward trend, although the current estimate shows a slight downturn. The growth in the proportion of people over sixty has been fairly dramatic since 1931, but unless there is a major decline in the birth rate this trend should level off. The proportion of old people has increased because of the improved survival of the relatively large proportion in the 0–19 age group earlier in the century.

Data

Figures for 1871–1971 are from the decennial census; those for 1976 are a mid-year estimate. Southern Ireland is included up to 1911, at which time its population was approximately 1½ million of each sex, but is excluded after independence in 1921. This year is omitted as no data for Northern Ireland was available and the 1931 Northern Ireland figures are estimates. No census was taken in 1941.

Sources

1871–1911: *Statistical Abstract for the UK*, No. 79
1931–1976: *Annual Abstract of Statistics*, 1977

Age and sex structure and growth of the UK population 1871-1976

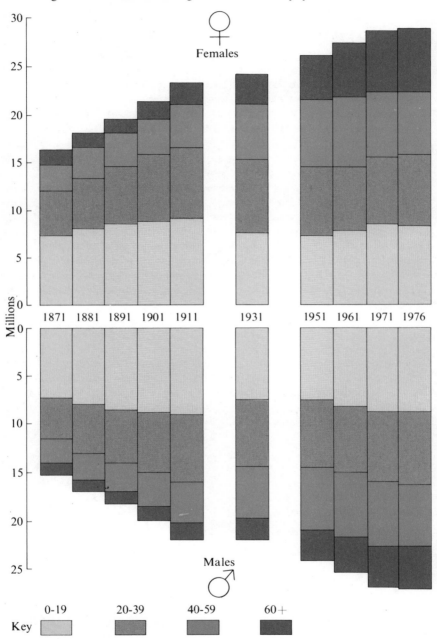

Females

Millions

1871 1881 1891 1901 1911   1931   1951 1961 1971 1976

Males

Key   0-19   20-39   40-59   60+

The crude birth rate is the number of live births in a given year expressed as a proportion (per thousand) of the total population. The graph opposite shows that, with the exception of the post-war years, the late 1950s and the early 1960s, the crude birth rate in the UK has been declining steadily since the turn of the century. This is a trend which has been evident in almost all industrialized societies.

There are many factors which can 'explain' the decline, including rising living standards, the changing role of women, urbanization and decreasing infant mortality, but the precise nature of their influence is not clearly understood. What is clear, however, is that the decline is due to behavioural rather than biological factors.

The table in the lower half of the page opposite shows recent trends in infant mortality (deaths of infants under one year of age) and in illegitimacy. By 1976, infant mortality had decreased to almost one-tenth of its 1900 level, and this has had an important influence on overall life expectancy (see topic 59). The illegitimacy rate, on the other hand, has more than doubled since 1900, so that now almost one of every ten births is illegitimate. Although the trend is provocative, general conclusions regarding behaviour patterns or social roles cannot be drawn from aggregate data such as this.

Data

As a measure of fertility, the crude birth rate must be interpreted with caution: since it is based on the total population, it is affected by changing age distribution within the population. A more specific measure of fertility is the number of births per 1,000 women aged 15–44, which has in fact exhibited the same trend as the crude birth rate over the period 1900–76.

Sources

Annual Abstracts of Statistics
Statistical Abstracts for the UK

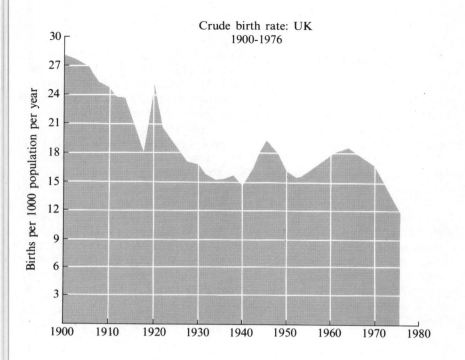

Crude birth rate: UK
1900-1976

Infant mortality rate and illegitimacy rate
for selected years: UK

	Deaths of infants under 1 year per 1000 live births	Illegitimate births as a percentage of all live births
1900-02	142	4.3
1910-12	110	4.5
1920-22	82	4.8
1930-32	67	4.8
1940-42	59	5.3
1950-52	30	5.0
1960-62	22	5.8
1970-72	18	8.2
1976	16	9.0

The bar chart allows comparison of the UK crude birth rate (live births per 1,000 population) with those of several other countries. The data are for 1975, or in some cases earlier, and illustrate clearly the strong association between increasing industrialization and decreasing birth rates. The industrialized nations, while differing widely in religious and social customs, have remarkably similar birth rates; the less developed nations, on the other hand, frequently have crude birth rates above 30 or 40. India does not have the highest birth rate by any means; those of Indonesia, Bangladesh, Brazil, Mexico and many others are higher.

Crude birth rate is not an accurate indicator of population growth, since the lack of industrialization that is associated with high birth rates is also frequently associated with high death rates, particularly infant mortality rates. A statistic which is used to indicate population growth is the natural increase rate, calculated by subtracting the crude death rate from the crude birth rate. It is interesting to note that in spite of their low birth rates, the industrialized nations on the chart all have positive rates of natural increase, with the exception of East and West Germany, which have slightly negative rates of increase.

Data

The same reservations regarding the interpretation of crude birth rates over time (see topic 57) hold when making cross-sectional comparisons between countries: the statistic will be affected by the age distribution of the population, and thus as a measure of fertility will not be as accurate as a birth rate based only upon the number of women of child-bearing age.

Source

United Nations Demographic Yearbook ˙

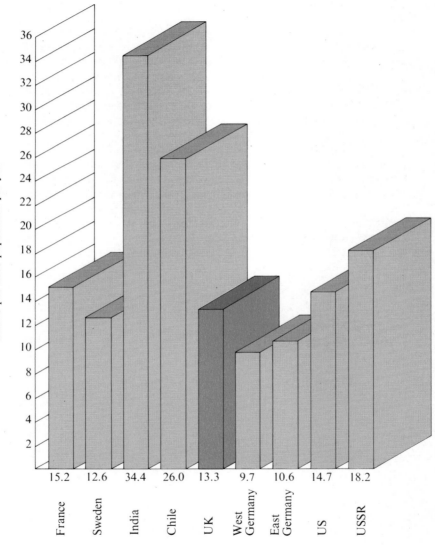

1975 Crude birth rates: International

Births per 1000 population per year

France	Sweden	India	Chile	UK	West Germany	East Germany	US	USSR
15.2	12.6	34.4	26.0	13.3	9.7	10.6	14.7	18.2

Life expectancy at birth is the average lifetime of persons born in a particular year. For recent years it must of course be a prediction, and the prediction is based on the death rates for people of various ages during the year.

The chart shows that life expectancy at birth has steadily increased since the turn of the century for both men and women, but that a man's life expectancy remains consistently lower than a woman's. In fact, the gap has been widening, a trend which is usually attributed to the effects of different environmental factors as opposed to innate biological differences. There is some evidence that the changing role of women in society may involve exposure to the detrimental factors affecting male mortality (e.g. stress) which may tend to reduce the gap in future.

The overall increase in life expectancy is largely due to a decrease in mortality in the younger ages, rather than to a general increase in lifespan. This is dramatically illustrated when we examine the age distribution of deaths in the two periods shown in the table opposite: in 1838–44 nearly half of all deaths were children under the age of 15. Another way of stating this is that the life expectancy of a person who has survived to the age of (say) 45 has increased very little since the turn of the century. (See topic 63: Death rates and 64: Infectious diseases.)

Sources

Annual Abstracts of Statistics
Statistical Abstracts for the UK
Trends in Mortality

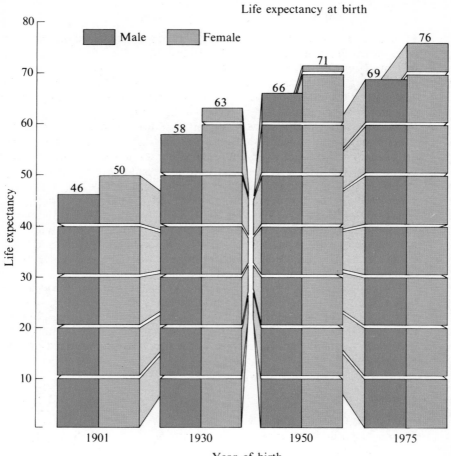

Life expectancy at birth

Age distribution of deaths (per cent)
1838-44, 1975

	Percentage of all deaths		
	0-14	15-64	over 65
1838-44	47	34	19
1975	2	23	75

The crude marriage rate (the number of marriages per 1,000 population) is an indicator of the rate of family formation. In the past the marriage rate has been considered a barometer of national prosperity, with high marriage rates coinciding with prosperous times and low rates with depression. The marriage rate is nowadays not explained so simply, but is considered to be related to such factors as age distribution of population, the divorce rate, and the role of women, in addition to economic factors.

With the exception of the sharp fluctuations surrounding the war years, the crude marriage rate has been remarkably stable since the turn of the century. In fact, the relatively flat graph opposite conceals two strong recent trends in marriage habits, namely a tendency for a greater *proportion* of the population to marry, and a tendency to marry at *younger ages.* Between 1931 and 1974 in England and Wales, the mean age at marriage for spinsters decreased from 25.5 to 22.7 years, while the percentage of women aged 45–9 who had never married decreased from 17 per cent to 7 per cent. Similar but less marked trends have been observed for males over this period.

The circular charts opposite illustrate a third recent trend, towards a larger proportion of civil weddings as opposed to church weddings. This is partly due to the increasing social acceptability of civil weddings, but, as the charts show, is largely due to the increasing proportion of marriages involving divorced persons, almost all of which are solemnized in civil ceremonies.

Sources

Annual Abstracts of Statistics
Leete, Richard, *Population Trends*, 3, Spring 1976, OPCS

Crude marriage rate: UK

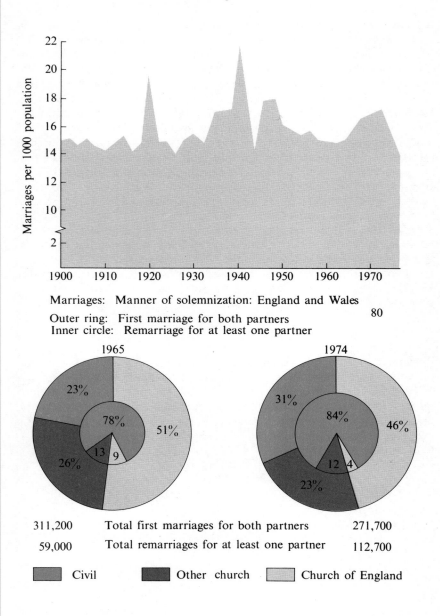

Marriages: Manner of solemnization: England and Wales

Outer ring: First marriage for both partners
Inner circle: Remarriage for at least one partner

80

1965

23%
78%
51%
13 9
26%

1974

31%
84%
46%
12 4
23%

311,200   Total first marriages for both partners   271,700

59,000   Total remarriages for at least one partner   112,700

■ Civil   ■ Other church   □ Church of England

A rising divorce rate has been a feature of British society ever since civil divorce became available in 1857. The rate has fluctuated coincidentally with war years and with changes in legislation regarding legal grounds for divorce or the financing of divorce litigation, but until the Second World War the number of divorces was always relatively insignificant. After the Second World War, however, the rate rose substantially to a peak in 1947, gradually subsiding to a low in 1960. It has risen almost continually since then to record and very significant levels in recent years.

The graph opposite shows the divorce rate (per 1,000 married couples) for the past two decades in England and Wales. The effects of the implementation of the Divorce Law Reform Act in 1971 are clearly evident: there was an initial short-term upsurge as a backlog of *de facto* broken marriages were terminated legally, followed by a more gradual long-term increase up to the present time.

Other trends over this time period were a gradual reduction in the mean age at divorce, reflecting the trend towards younger age at marriage (see topic 60), and a reduction in the duration of marriage. The grounds for divorce granted have also changed markedly, as illustrated in the circular charts opposite, reflecting more likely the changes in legal grounds for divorce than any significant changes in marriage behaviour.

Data

Because it is based on the married population only, the divorce rate presented here is a more accurate indicator of family stability than the crude divorce rate often used (base upon the entire population). It must be remembered, however, that any divorce rate measures only *de jure* broken marriages which will be some proportion of *de facto* broken marriages, and what proportion this is must be determined from other than routine data.

Sources

Annual Abstracts of Statistics
Registrar General's Statistical Review, England and Wales
Leete, Richard, *Population Trends*, 3, Spring 1976, OPCS

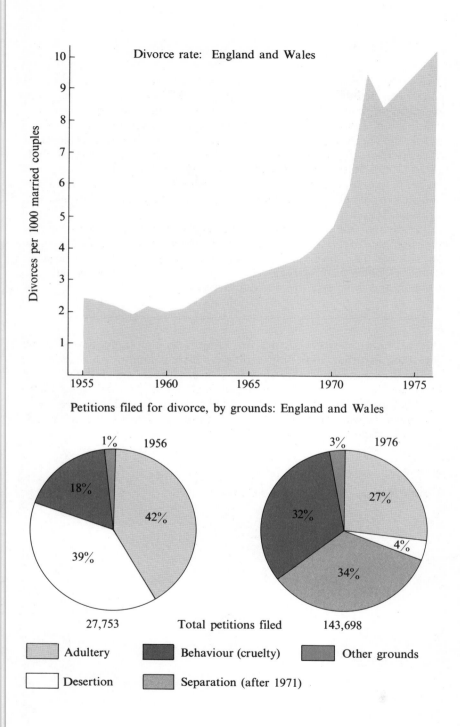

Divorce rate: England and Wales

Divorces per 1000 married couples

Petitions filed for divorce, by grounds: England and Wales

1%   1956

18%

42%

39%

27,753   Total petitions filed   143,698

3%   1976

32%

27%

4%

34%

☐ Adultery   ■ Behaviour (cruelty)   ☐ Other grounds

☐ Desertion   ☐ Separation (after 1971)

The chart opposite shows recent crude divorce rates for selected countries, including England and Wales. The crude divorce rate is an indicator of family breakups, but it must be interpreted with some caution, since as shown in topic 61 the divorce rate is quite sensitive to changes in legislation. Thus, a low divorce rate may well be an indication of restrictive legislation rather than of family stability. It is possible that *de facto* family breakups (including separations, desertions, etc.) are higher in countries with restrictive divorce legislation, but that cannot be deduced from the data provided here. The figures are for 1974 or in some cases earlier.

The divorce rate in England and Wales falls about midway between the very high rate of the USA and Sweden and the very low rate of Italy. Italy does not in fact have the lowest divorce rate since there are several countries which have no legal provision for divorce, such as Brazil and Ireland, and thus have divorce rates of zero.

Data

International divorce statistics are subject to the same reservations regarding accuracy and comparability as international birth rates, with the additional complication that divorce is a procedure defined under local civil law, and is thus more difficult to standardize than birth statistics. All of the data presented opposite is considered to be complete and accurate, with the possible exception of the data for the USA and Italy, which must be regarded as provisional.

Source

United Nations Demographic Yearbook

Crude divorce rates:

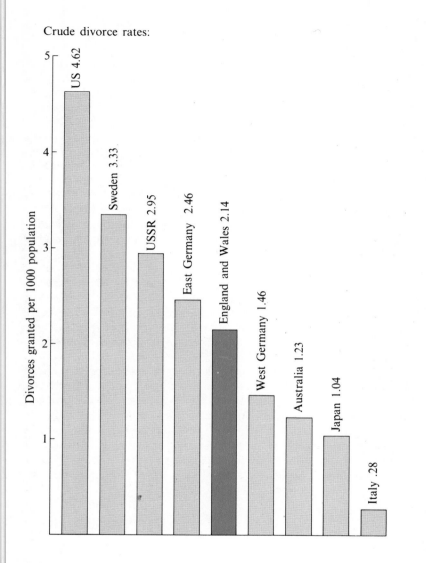

Divorces granted per 1000 population

US 4.62
Sweden 3.33
USSR 2.95
East Germany 2.46
England and Wales 2.14
West Germany 1.46
Australia 1.23
Japan 1.04
Italy .28

The top graph shows the change in the crude death rate for males and females in Britain from 1870 to 1976. There is a sharp decline in the periods 1870–80 and 1890–1920, followed by a slower decline up to 1960. Most of the decline in the death rates occurred before the advances of modern medicine. Currently, the trend is slowly reversing. The age structure of the population has also changed over the period (cf. topic 56), so standardized death rates would show a larger decrease.

The pie charts show that the two major causes of death in 1851, infectious and tubercular diseases, were already less important by 1911 and are now responsible for less than 2 per cent of all deaths. The early part of this decrease can be attributed mainly to improvements in the living conditions and general health of the population. Effective treatments and vaccines for most of these diseases did not emerge until after 1935.

Diseases of the nervous system appear to have declined, but this is largely due to changes in diagnosis and classification as these diseases become better understood. About half the deaths in this category in 1851 were loosely diagnosed as due to convulsions; specific causes of death included insanity and delirium tremens! The disappearance of the category 'old age' also reflects a change in recording, with more emphasis placed on diagnosing some final cause.

The chart for 1976 shows clearly why heart disease and cancer are referred to as the modern killers. The two main causes of death are ischaemic heart diseases (such as arteriosclerosis and coronary-thrombosis) and lung cancer. Some of the increase may be due to improved diagnosis and longer life spans that give these diseases time to emerge, but several aspects of modern life, such as smoking, diet and lack of exercise, are known to increase the risk from these diseases. Respiratory diseases, especially pneumonia, have remained a major problem despite available drug therapy.

Data

The death rates for 1870–1970 are an average for the three-year period covering each census year. 1940 is omitted as no census was taken. The 1976 figure is specific to that year. The cause of death data for 1851 is for England and Wales only. The classification of diseases has changed over the period, but the trends remain fairly clear.

Sources

Registrar General of England and Wales Annual Report, 1855
Statistical Abstract for the UK, Nos. 70, 79
Annual Abstract of Statistics, 1977

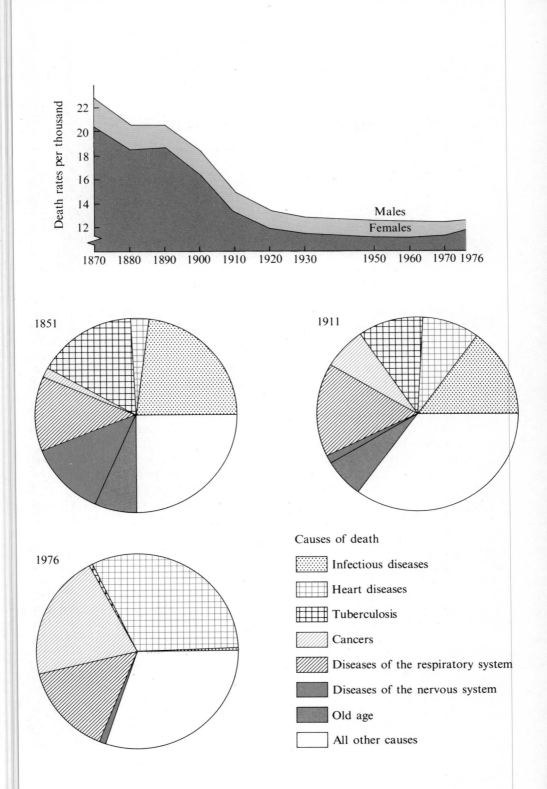

Death rates per thousand

Males

Females

1870 1880 1890 1900 1910 1920 1930 1950 1960 1970 1976

1851

1911

1976

Causes of death

Infectious diseases

Heart diseases

Tuberculosis

Cancers

Diseases of the respiratory system

Diseases of the nervous system

Old age

All other causes

The graphs show the number of notified cases in Britain for a selection of infectious diseases. They illustrate the fact that the reduction in deaths from these diseases (cf. topic 63) is due not only to improved treatment, but also to a reduction in cases.

Whooping cough, once described by Chinese physicians as the 'hundred days' cough', is one of the more common notifiable diseases and is probably under-reported, particularly in its mild form. There is no specific treatment, but a vaccine was introduced in the 1930s, although no major impact was made until post-war trials had proved its efficacy.

Scarlet fever is the only disease presented here for which there is no immunization available. The substantial fall in cases is due partly to effective treatment restricting the spread of disease, but the main factor is an unexplained reduction in virulence. In the nineteenth century, when it was often a fatal disease, scarlet fever was a jocular description of a fondness for soldiers (red coats).

Epidemics of poliomyelitis were common as recently as the 1950s. It was a particularly serious problem as there was, and is, no specific treatment. Death or paralysis were frequent outcomes, but the introduction of the Salk, and later Sabin, vaccines have virtually eliminated the disease.

The dramatic fall in the number of cases of diphtheria between 1941 and 1951 suggests the possible importance of immunization. A national campaign was launched in 1940 and this disease is now rather rare.

Tuberculosis was the most common of the infectious diseases notified in 1976. Most cases were respiratory, caused by inhaling the tubercule germ, but tuberculosis can occur in many parts of the body if infected material is ingested. The number of cases has been substantially reduced by stricter food controls, mass X-ray screening to detect presymptomatic cases and, in particular, the introduction of the BCG vaccination in 1954.

Data

All 1921 figures and the 1931 figure for tuberculosis exclude Northern Ireland. Notifications for Northern Ireland are recorded from 1923, but the notification of tuberculosis was not compulsory in all districts until after 1931. The number of cases is small in relation to the total and so does not distort the presentation. Different time periods have been used because the diseases reported are changed at various times.

Sources

Annual Abstract of Statistics, 1935–46, 1958, 1966, 1977
Statistical Abstract for the UK, no. 79

Notifications of infectious diseases

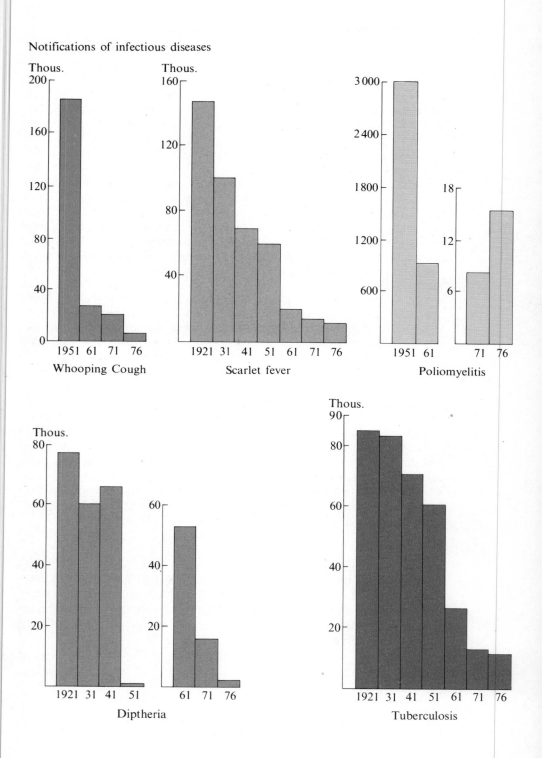

Whooping Cough

Scarlet fever

Poliomyelitis

Diptheria

Tuberculosis

The line graphs show the number of reported suicides per million of population in England and Wales from 1916 to 1976. Suicides are under-reported, as it is often difficult to distinguish suicides from accidental deaths. Accidental poisonings and single vehicle crashes with no passengers may conceal suicides.

The suicide rate for males is consistently higher than that for females, although the current difference is smaller than at the beginning of the period. The graph for males shows a sharp increase from 1916, through the depression years, peaking in 1936. There is a smaller peak in 1956, then a steady decline. The female graph peaks later, 1956–66, and then also declines. The methods of suicide recorded here account for almost all the female suicides, but there are a number of unrecorded male suicides by violent methods such as firearms and cutting and piercing instruments.

The graphs for suicides by gassing follow a trend similar to that of totals. The increase at the beginning of the period may reflect more domestic use of gas, but the decline starts before the introduction of non-toxic North Sea Gas in 1967. The increase in other poisonings after the Second World War is due mainly to drug abuse, and the current reversal of the trend may represent changes in prescription behaviour and over-the-counter sales because of the abuse problem. This category is likely to be under-reported, as noted above, and any increase in this phenomenon will bias the overall trend. The hanging category, which includes strangulation and suffocation, increases between 1966 and 1976 for no clear reason, unless other methods were becoming more difficult. Suicides by drowning have declined steadily.

The bar graphs show occupational mortality ratios for suicides in 1961. The data are difficult to interpret as the occupation taken from the death certificate is that undertaken immediately prior to death and may be affected by the factors causing the suicide. The industrial occupations all have low ratios, as do the 'white collar' categories. Sport and recreation is surprisingly high, but perhaps there are a lot of bad losers!

Data

Some changes have been made in the categories of suicide that are recorded and there is now a separate category for possible but unproven suicides. The occupational data is for males aged between 15 and 65, standardized for age and sex. 100 represents the overall standardized death rate for suicide.

Sources

Registrar General's Statistical Review of England and Wales, 1961, 1966
OPCS Monitor, 1978
Registrar General's Decennial Supplement, England and Wales, 1961

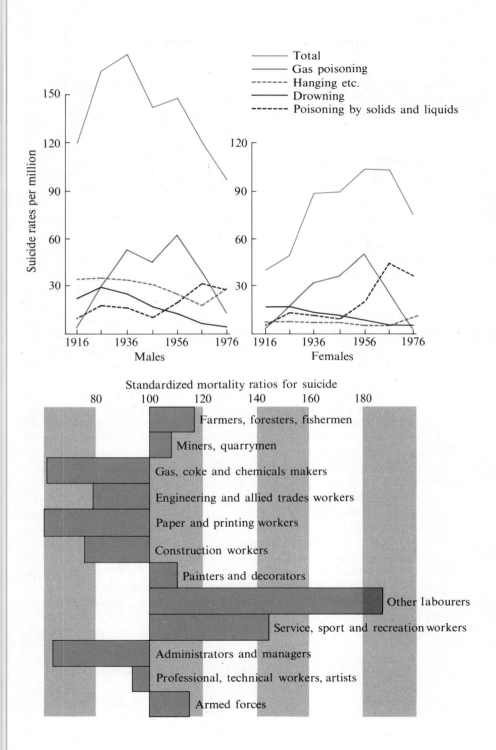

Suicide rates per million

Total
Gas poisoning
Hanging etc.
Drowning
Poisoning by solids and liquids

Males

Females

Standardized mortality ratios for suicide

Farmers, foresters, fishermen
Miners, quarrymen
Gas, coke and chemicals makers
Engineering and allied trades workers
Paper and printing workers
Construction workers
Painters and decorators
Other labourers
Service, sport and recreation workers
Administrators and managers
Professional, technical workers, artists
Armed forces

The graph shows the suicide rate per 100,000 population for various countries, 1972–74. Cross-section data are often studied to investigate the possibility that some underlying national characteristics may affect the suicide rate. A casual inspection of this data would suggest that religion might be a protective factor, with Northern Ireland, Italy and Israel having very low suicide rates. Czechoslovakia has the highest rate, followed by Sweden and then the stronger industrial countries, Germany, Japan and the USA. The UK countries have moderate suicide rates despite the current economic gloom.

Interpretation of international data is not, however, straightforward. Czechoslovakia is included to represent Eastern Europe, but is not entirely typical. Several countries did not report separate suicide figures; of those that did, Hungary also has a very high suicide rate but Bulgaria and Yugoslavia, for instance, have more moderate rates. In contrast to Sweden's high rate, Norway has a fairly low rate; this might reflect differences in temperament and social climate between the two countries.

Considering the religious aspect, predominantly Catholic countries not reported here also have fairly low rates, but it is not certain that the Catholic church acts as a preventive agent. It may be that suicides are more carefully disguised by both victims and family because of the stigma attached.

Some variation in suicide rates will be accounted for by differing procedures for determining the cause of death in possible suicide cases and different methods of recording deaths. For example, in England Wales an autopsy is performed in all cases of violent death and cause of death is determined by a coroner's court, whilst in Germany a doctor alone can certify death as suicide and in Czechoslovakia and Japan the decision is partly made by the police.

Recording suicides presents more difficulties. In many cases a decision is not reached but suicide is suspected. In Japan and Czechoslovakia these are included with suicides if this is the most probable cause of death. Other countries record them as accidental, suicide being not proven, undetermined or unknown. This tends to inflate the figures for Japan and Czechoslovakia. A category for deaths from self-inflicted injury where intention is not determined has now been introduced in the international classifications and this should improve comparability if widely adopted.

Data

The figures are for different years because of variations in data availability. Problems of comparability are discussed above.

Source

United Nations Demographic Yearbook

Suicide rates per 100,000 population

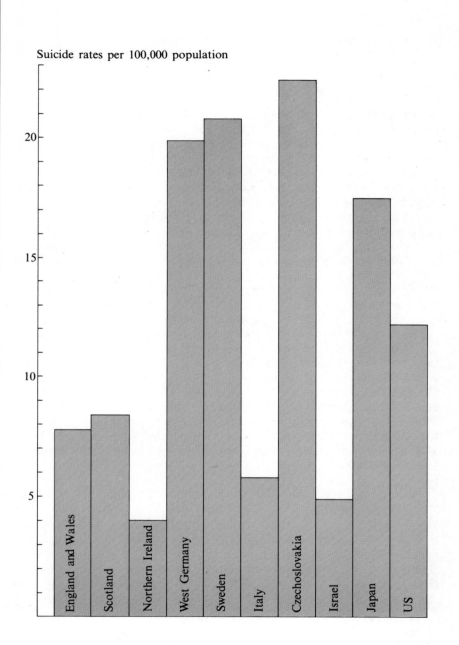

The graphs show the average net migration of population in the intercensal periods from 1871 to 1976. The only period in which there has been a net gain of population in the UK is in the period 1931–61. The higher net gain shown for England and Wales in the same period emphasizes the fact that much of the migration from Scotland and Northern Ireland is into England.

The UK figures show a small peak towards the end of the nineteenth century and near the end of Britain's expansionary period as a colonial power. The largest loss of population occurs at the beginning of the twentieth century, continuing into the Depression, probably as people emigrated to seek better prospects in the Americas, Australia and New Zealand. The Depression continued in the 1930s, but the gain in population in this period may be accounted for by the build-up towards war on the Continent and a consequent influx of refugees. Substantial immigration carried on in the post-war period and was encouraged as the economy picked up. Since the 1960s the trend has reversed again, so to some extent the pattern of migration reflects the state of the economy.

The disaggregated data is complicated by inter-regional movements. The figures for England and Wales are always of the same sign as those of the UK. Scotland and Northern Ireland both exhibit a continuous loss of population. The rate of loss will be influenced by similar factors to those affecting the UK and also by the relative state of the economy in England and Wales. Emigration from Scotland increased in the 1950s and 1960s when employment prospects were relatively good over the border, but has decreased as North Sea oil has begun to provide more on-shore jobs. The increased emigration from Northern Ireland in the 1970s is most likely to be due to the escalation of the civil strife.

Data

The interpretation of trends is made more difficult because the figures are only averages and the exact timing of changes cannot be detected. A twenty-year average is given for 1931–51 as no census was taken in 1941. It should be remembered that the populations of Scotland and Northern Ireland are about ten times smaller than that of England and Wales, so the loss of population in these countries is proportionately greater.

Source

Annual Abstract of Statistics, 1935–46, 1977

Average net migration of population (thousands)

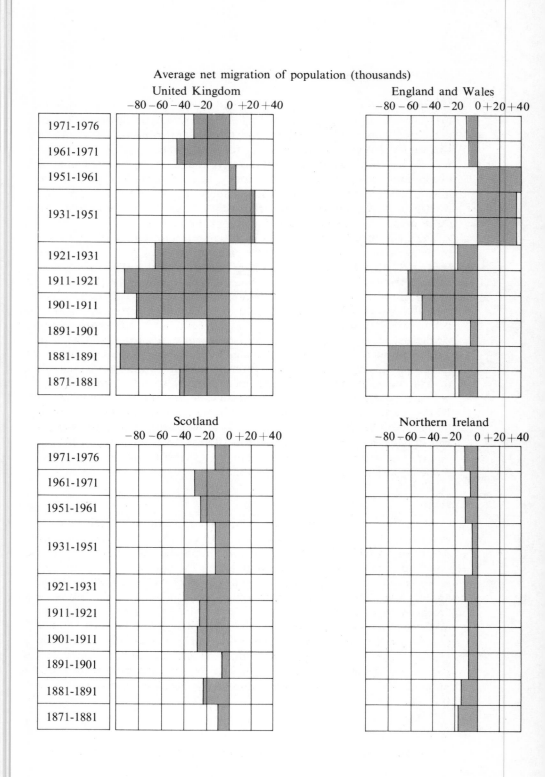

In this topic, the distribution of personal sector wealth in Great Britain (as distinct from the United Kingdom) is examined. Two graphs are presented opposite: the upper relates to the distribution of wealth in England and Wales, while the lower relates to all of Great Britain. (The reason for the separate presentations is that a longer run of data is available for England and Wales alone). In each of the two graphs, the lower line portrays the percentage share of wealth owned by the wealthiest 1 per cent of people, the second from the bottom shows the share owned by the wealthiest 5 per cent, and so on.

The clear impression gained from these graphs is that the share owned by the wealthier groups (whether the richest 1 per cent, 5 per cent, 10 per cent or 20 per cent) has been declining steadily over the years since 1923. Indeed, the wealthiest 1 per cent owned 60.9 per cent of the total wealth in 1923, but by 1972 this share had almost halved—falling to 31.7 per cent of the wealth. Between 1923 and 1972, the share owned by the top 5 per cent fell from 82 per cent to 56 per cent, while the share of the wealthiest 10 per cent fell from 89.1 per cent to 70.4 per cent. (These figures all relate to England and Wales.) Clearly, the tendency has been for an increasingly equal distribution of wealth through time (though there have been some interesting 'hiccups' in this general pattern).

The gap between the 'top 20 per cent' line and the horizontal line at 100 per cent indicates the share owned by the *least wealthy* 80 per cent of the population. This share has manifestly grown through time: in England and Wales it rose from 5.8 per cent in 1923 to 15.1 per cent in 1972; in Great Britain, it rose from 8.4 per cent in 1938 to 14.7 per cent owned by the least wealthy 80 per cent in 1972.

Data

Considerable controversies rage over the appropriate definition of wealth. Such arguments are examined and appraised in the book by Atkinson and Harrison (below) from which the data portrayed was obtained; many commentators think this is the best source of unbiased information on the topic. (Of the many possibilities explored by these authors, their findings with regard to pension rights—not included above—are of interest. These findings suggest that the inclusion of these rights might decrease the share owned by the top 10% by some half a percentage point in 1938 but by 4 percentage points in 1972. This tentative 'correction factor' is clearly growing in importance, albeit at a modest $\frac{1}{10}$ per cent per year.) (A wealth of other detail can be obtained from the various publications of the *Royal Commission on the Distribution of Income and Wealth.*)

Source

Atkinson, A. B. and Harrison, A. J., *Distribution of Personal Wealth in Britain*

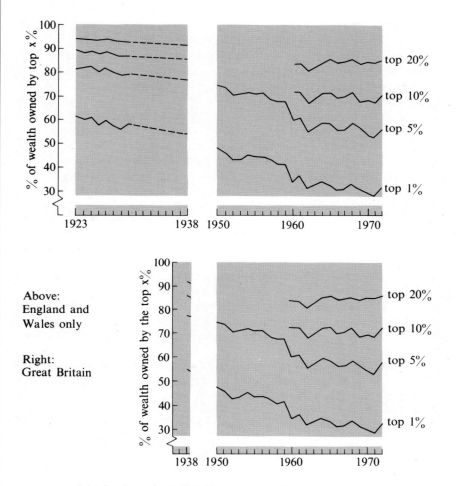

Above:
England and
Wales only

Right:
Great Britain

Distribution of wealth among men and among women -
England and Wales 1970

	Share of top x% of men in total wealth owned by man	Share of top x% of women in total wealth owned by women
Top 1%	27.7	32.1
Top 5%	50.0	58.1
Top 10%	63.9	72.9
Mean wealth	£3348 per man	£1980 per woman

This topic examines the distribution of personal incomes over the population in Britain, both before and after tax, and discusses how these distributions have changed through time. The technique of visual presentation used on the opposite page is known as the *Lorenz* curve; possibly a few words of explanation of this technique would prove useful.

For each of the four years portrayed, the outer curve represents the pre-tax distribution of income, while the inner curve represents the post-tax distribution. Some of the data portrayed is given numerically in the table at the foot of the page; thus, for example, the outer (pre-tax) curve for 1949 shows that the top 1 per cent of income earners earned 11.2 per cent of the total income, the top 10 per cent earned (between them) 33.2 per cent (= 11.2 + 22.0) of the total income, the top 20 per cent earned 47.3 per cent of the total income, and so on. Now, if everyone had exactly the same income, then the 'top 1 per cent' would earn 1 per cent of the total income, the 'top 10 per cent' would earn 10 per cent, and so on . . .; in this case the 'distribution' would be represented by the straight line joining the bottom left-hand corner to the right-hand top corner. Therefore, the divergence of the *actual* distribution from the completely equal distribution is represented by the divergence of the actual curve from this straight line; these divergencies are shaded in the diagram.

Two things are apparent from these diagrams. First, the post-tax distribution is more equal than the pre-tax distribution for each of the four years (though the difference is not particularly pronounced, except for the year 1949). Secondly, it is very difficult for the eye to detect any significant changes in the distribution of income over time; indeed, any changes that took place have clearly been on a relatively modest scale. A measure (more sensitive than the naked eye) is the *Gini coefficient*: this measures the area of the shaded part as a percentage of the area of the triangle below the diagonal. Clearly, the smaller this coefficient is, the more nearly equal the distribution. As far as pre-tax incomes are concerned, the Gini coefficient was 41.1 per cent in 1949, 37.4 per cent in 1968/69 (a Labour government), 38.3 per cent in 1971/72 (a Conservative government) and 36.6 per cent in 1975/76 (a Labour government). The corresponding post-tax Gini coefficients were 35.5 per cent, 33.2 per cent, 34.2 per cent and 31.5 per cent.

Data

It should be noted that the post-tax distribution refers only to income tax and social security taxation and transfers. Thus, the post-tax representation can not be construed as a picture of the *post-budget* distribution.

Source

Economic Trends, May 1978

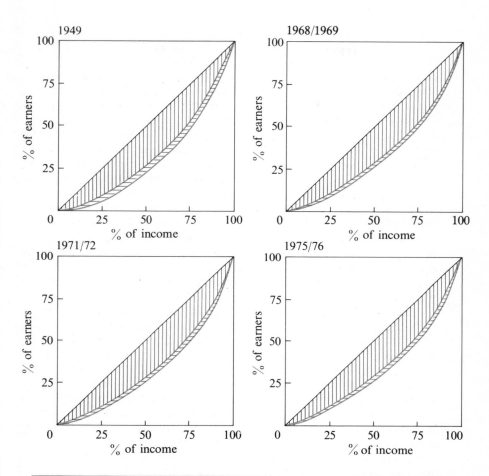

Percentage shares of income					
	Quantile group	1949	1968/69	1971/72	1975/76
	top 1%	11.2	7.1	6.5	5.6
Pre-tax	2-10%	22.0	20.0	20.8	20.2
	11-20%	14.1	15.4	15.9	16.1
	21-50%	29.0	33.3	33.4	33.8
	51-100%	23.7	24.2	23.4	24.3
	top 1%	6.4	4.6	4.6	3.6
	2-10%	20.7	19.0	19.5	18.7
Post-tax	11-20%	14.5	15.5	15.9	15.8
	21-50%	31.9	34.3	34.1	34.5
	51-100%	26.5	26.6	25.9	27.4

70 RELATIVE PURCHASING POWER OF 1938 AND 1976 INCOMES

One of the main problems in comparing incomes over a relatively long time period is that variables such as the rate of inflation, the number of hours worked per week and increases in money wage rates make direct comparisons of the relative affluence of consumers in the two time periods very difficult. This discussion attempts to get round some of these problems by expressing the relative purchasing power of each year's average earnings in terms of the amount of time the person with the average weekly earnings had to work in order to earn enough to purchase given quantities of certain basic foodstuffs.

Two alternative comparisons are contained in the picture opposite. The first is given by the unbracketed figures; these show the number of minutes that a man with the average level of earnings had to work, in each of the two years, in order to buy the stated item; *these figures ignore the effect of tax*. Thus, for example, the average British worker had to work 11.6 minutes in 1938 to be able to buy a pint of milk; by 1976, he had to work just 3.2 minutes.

The bracketed figures carry out the same comparison—but this time on *net* rather than *gross* earnings. In 1976, the average earner was forced to pay 24½ per cent of his gross pay in the form of income tax and national insurance contributions: thus, in order to earn one minute's worth of net pay, he had to work for 1.324 minutes. In 1938, the position was considerably different: the man on average earnings (if married, as the above analysis has assumed) paid *no* income tax at all; the only deduction was 1s 7d per week in (the then equivalent of) national insurance contributions. Thus, to earn one minute's worth of net pay, he had to work just 1.023 minutes.

Nevertheless, the 1976 worker is still clearly considerably better off than his 1938 counterpart.

Data

The earnings figures are for full-time manual men over the age of 21. The tax figures assume a married man with two children under the age of 11. National average food prices are assumed throughout.

Sources

Household Food Consumption and Expenditure
British Labour Statistics Historical Abstract
New Earnings Surveys
Annual Abstract of Statistics

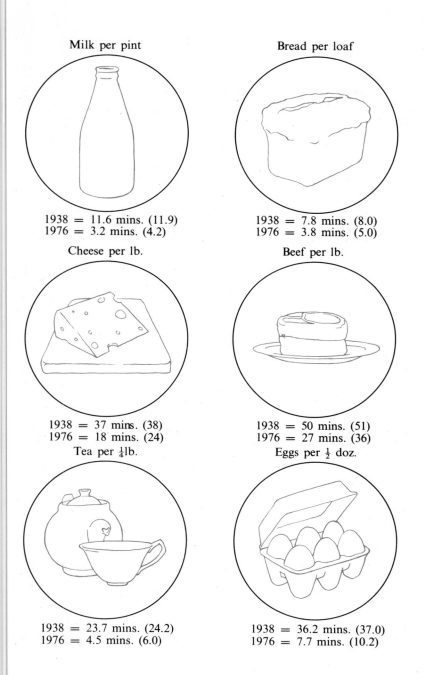

Milk per pint

1938 = 11.6 mins. (11.9)
1976 = 3.2 mins. (4.2)

Bread per loaf

1938 = 7.8 mins. (8.0)
1976 = 3.8 mins. (5.0)

Cheese per lb.

1938 = 37 mins. (38)
1976 = 18 mins. (24)

Beef per lb.

1938 = 50 mins. (51)
1976 = 27 mins. (36)

Tea per $\frac{1}{4}$lb.

1938 = 23.7 mins. (24.2)
1976 = 4.5 mins. (6.0)

Eggs per $\frac{1}{2}$ doz.

1938 = 36.2 mins. (37.0)
1976 = 7.7 mins. (10.2)

The introduction of the *New Earnings Survey* by the Department of Employment enables a comparison of earnings by *occupation* to be carried out. Unfortunately, however, data on a consistent basis is available only for the period 1973 to 1977. However, some interesting analyses are available—particularly as this period was a significant one in Britain's recent economic history.

The left-hand diagram portrays the average earnings of full-time male employees over the age of 21, for April 1973 and for April 1977, broken down by occupation. The occupational classes used are as follows:

1 Managerial (general management)
2 Professional and related supporting management and administration (this class includes accountants, systems analysts, executives, and the like)
3 Professional and related in education, welfare and health (mainly teachers, but also including welfare workers and nurse administrators)
4 Professional and related in science, engineering, technology and similar fields (including scientists and engineers)
5 Managerial (excluding general management)
6 Clerical and related
7 Selling
8 Security and protective service (including policemen, firemen and security guards)
9 Catering, cleaning, hairdressing and other personal service
10 Farming, fishing and related
11 Materials processing (excluding metals)
12 Making and repairing (excluding metal and electrical)
13 Processing, making, repairing and related (metal and electrical)
14 Painting, repetitive assembling, product inspecting, packaging and related
15 Construction, mining and related not identified elsewhere
16 Transport operating, materials and storing and related.
(Groups 1 to 8 are classified as *non-manual*, 9 to 16 as *manual*.)

The right-hand diagram shows the percentage increases in earnings over the four years from April 1973 to April 1977. The table below gives all the pictured information, as well as the fact that the retail price index rose 96 per cent over this period.

The facts essentially speak for themselves. However, it is interesting to note that those occupations which were above average in earnings in 1973 remained so in 1977; likewise, those with below average earnings in 1973 remained so in 1977. Nevertheless, there was a general tendency for those with above-average earnings in 1973 to experience below-average percentage increases in the four years to 1977.

Source

New Earnings Survey

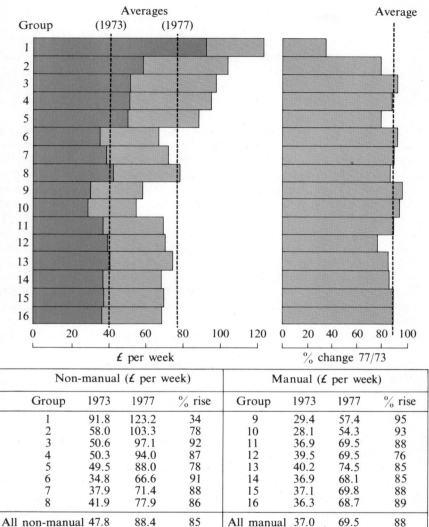

Non-manual (£ per week)				Manual (£ per week)			
Group	1973	1977	% rise	Group	1973	1977	% rise
1	91.8	123.2	34	9	29.4	57.4	95
2	58.0	103.3	78	10	28.1	54.3	93
3	50.6	97.1	92	11	36.9	69.5	88
4	50.3	94.0	87	12	39.5	69.5	76
5	49.5	88.0	78	13	40.2	74.5	85
6	34.8	66.6	91	14	36.9	68.1	85
7	37.9	71.4	88	15	37.1	69.8	88
8	41.9	77.9	86	16	36.3	68.7	89
All non-manual	47.8	88.4	85	All manual	37.0	69.5	88
All workers	40.9	76.8	88	All workers	40.9	76.8	88
Retail price index			96	Retail price index			96

An international comparison of rates of personal income taxation is the concern of this topic. Although such comparisons are rather hazardous (due to differences in taxation systems in different countries), some broad generalizations can be drawn. In particular, support for the view that personal incomes are taxed relatively highly in the United Kingdom can be found.

On the uppper diagram, the income tax thresholds and the initial rate of income tax are plotted for each of ten countries. As is apparent, the further to the left is the country's dot, the lower the income at which the individual begins to pay tax; moreover, the nearer the top of the page is the country's dot, the higher is the initial rate. Clearly, taxation in the UK is relatively severe in both these respects. (Indeed, no country anywhere in the world has a starting rate as high as the UK's 35 per cent.)

The lower diagram portrays the position at the opposite end of the income scale—the maximum tax rate, and the point at which it begins to be applied. Once again, the further to the left or the higher on the page is a country's dot, the more severe is the highest rate of taxation. Clearly, the situation in the UK is particularly severe. Indeed, only five countries in the world had—in 1976—a higher top rate than that of the UK; these were Algeria (100 per cent), Egypt (96.6 per cent), Tanzania (95 per cent), Japan (83.7 per cent inclusive of local income taxes), and Portugal (84 per cent). It is interesting to note that the top Italian rate (72 per cent) is applied only to incomes in excess of £381,550—a threshold almost 18 times higher than the UK threshold.

Data

The data relates to the tax position of a married man with two children, with entirely earned income. (Unearned income may carry a further supplement.) The sterling equivalents are calculated using the exchange rates prevailing at 8 March 1976. The dots and figures *in brackets* show rates inclusive of representative local income tax, or of general additional charge. The (differing) dates for which the information is given should be carefully noted.

Source

Hansard

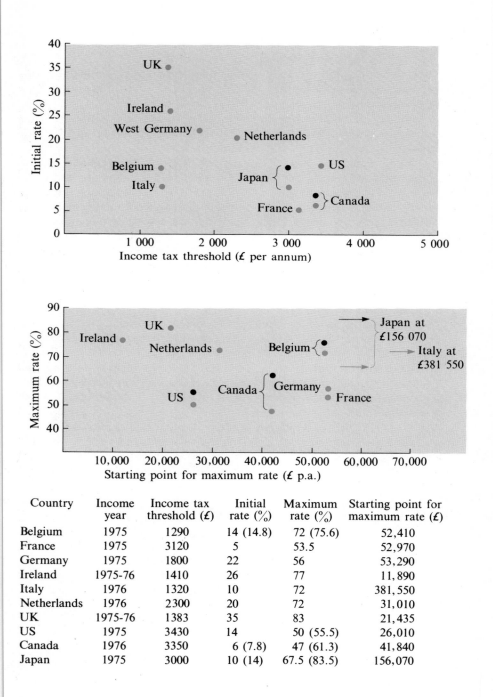

Country	Income year	Income tax threshold (£)	Initial rate (%)	Maximum rate (%)	Starting point for maximum rate (£)
Belgium	1975	1290	14 (14.8)	72 (75.6)	52,410
France	1975	3120	5	53.5	52,970
Germany	1975	1800	22	56	53,290
Ireland	1975-76	1410	26	77	11,890
Italy	1976	1320	10	72	381,550
Netherlands	1976	2300	20	72	31,010
UK	1975-76	1383	35	83	21,435
US	1975	3430	14	50 (55.5)	26,010
Canada	1976	3350	6 (7.8)	47 (61.3)	41,840
Japan	1975	3000	10 (14)	67.5 (83.5)	156,070

The effects of income taxation (and other compulsory deductions) on personal incomes can be analysed in a variety of ways; in this topic two such ways are examined.

One way is to take a particular UK salary figure, and calculate what proportion of that income would have to be paid in income tax in different countries (converting the salary into foreign currencies by using the prevailing exchange rate). This analysis is carried out in the upper diagram for three different income levels: (1) UK average earnings; (2) twice UK average earnings; and (3) thrice UK average earnings. It will be noted that in four of the nine countries portrayed (namely Belgium, France, Germany and the Netherlands) *no tax* would be payable on an income equal to UK average earnings. However, in the UK itself, 13.1 per cent of that income would be payable in income tax. As is apparent from this diagram, a higher proportion of income is paid in the form of income tax in the UK than in any other country at all three levels of income (with the sole exception of Ireland's proportion for earning levels of three times the average).

However, this analysis could be considered 'unfair' insofar as an income equal to the UK average (when converted at official exchange rates) would be considered a relatively low income in the more affluent countries (such as Germany and the United States). One way to avoid this problem is to compare the tax positions of workers earning *the average amount relative to their own countries*. This analysis is presented in the lower diagram for the years 1972 and 1974. It shows, for example, that the worker earning the Belgian average earnings in 1972 would pay 19 per cent of his income in (Belgian) tax, whereas the French average earner would pay 8 per cent in (French) tax. It will be noted that (as expected) the UK position—at 19 per cent—looks less severe in this analysis.

Data

The analysis assumes a married man with two children. The upper diagram is based on the March 1978 figure for the average earnings of all full-time workers aged 18 and over. The tax rates are generally those for 1978. The lower diagram covers both income tax and social security deductions, whereas the upper diagram covers income tax deductions alone.

Sources

OECD *Revenue Statistics* 1964–75
Hansard

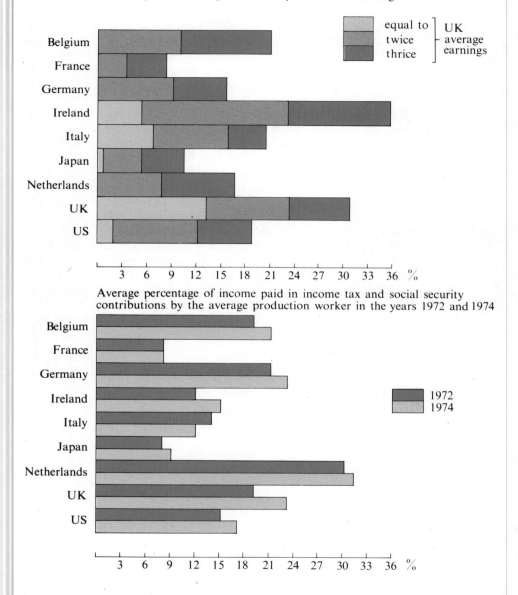

Percentage of income paid in tax by those with earnings

Average percentage of income paid in income tax and social security contributions by the average production worker in the years 1972 and 1974

Our income tax system is progressive. That is, the higher the income earned, the greater the proportion of it that is paid in tax. This effect is obtained by the device whereby higher rates of tax are charged on incremental income bands. This section examines the rates of tax, and the income increments that they are charged on, for the tax years 1953/54 and 1976/77.

The data is portrayed in bar chart form, with rates of tax on the vertical axis, and the income band along the horizontal axis. For both years, a portion of income earned is tax-free (the single person's allowance). Thereafter, tax is paid at higher rates. However, it should be remembered that the higher rates are paid only on the income increment: thus, in 1976/77 a single person earning £6,500 p.a. would pay no tax on the first £735, 35 per cent on the income up to £5,000, 40 per cent on the next £500 and 45 per cent on the £1,000 after that—a total payment of tax of £2,142.75, an effective overall rate of almost 33 per cent.

Comparing the tax years 1953/54 and 1976/77, it would appear that the high income earner has had a considerable easing of his tax burden. Not only is the exemption limit higher, but also the rates at which tax is paid are in every case lower, with the maximum rate paid being reduced from 95 per cent to 83 per cent. However, this is largely a false picture, in that incomes have increased during this period to the extent that more people are paying higher marginal rates of tax. If the income bands are deflated, by dividing by the increase in real wages (see topic 77), then it can be seen that although tax rates are lower, the bands have not been increased to compensate for inflation, and many more people are affected by higher marginal rates of taxation.

Data

Income tax rates (assuming single person).

Source

Annual Abstract of Statistics

Tax year 1953/54

Tax year 1976/77

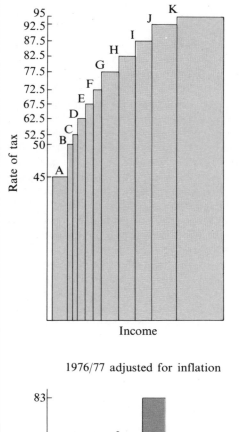

1976/77 adjusted for inflation

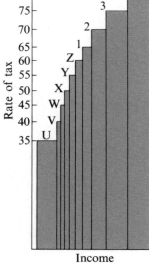

A	=	up to	£2 000
B	=	2 000	2 500
C	=	2 500	3 000
D	=	3 000	4 000
E	=	4 000	5 000
F	=	5 000	6 000
G	=	6 000	8 000
H	=	8 000	10,000
I	=	10,000	12,000
J	=	12,000	15,000
K	=	15,000	20,000
L	=	up to	5 000
M	=	5 000	5 500
N	=	5 500	6 500
O	=	6 500	7 500
P	=	7 500	8 500
Q	=	8 500	10,000
R	=	10,000	12,000
S	=	12,000	15,000
T	=	15,000	20,000
U	=	up to	2 913
V	=	2 913	3 205
W	=	3 205	3 788
X	=	3 788	4 371
Y	=	4 371	4 953
Z	=	4 953	5 828
1	=	5 828	6 993
2	=	6 993	8 741
3	=	8 741	11,655

An international comparison of the relative affluence (or impoverishment) of workers in the UK with those of our major competitors, France, West Germany, Italy, the US and Japan, must inevitably involve comparisons of real earnings rates, that is, earnings adjusted for the effects of inflation. This section is concerned with comparing the increases in real wages of each country since 1953.

To make this comparison, an index of wages in manufacturing industry and an index of retail prices, both with a base year of 1953 (= 100) were compiled. Then, to show the growth of real wages the earnings index was divided by the price index, to give a real wage index. In order to demonstrate in a clear manner the relative growth of real wages, the values of the real wage index for two years, 1966 and 1975, were taken and arranged in the form of a bar chart. Remembering that each country had an equal value of real wage index in 1953 (= 100), it can be seen that the value of the real wage index for these years represents the growth in real wages during this time period. In 1966 the growth in real earnings was approximately equal, with West Germany leading the growth table. However, by 1975 a more marked inequality had emerged, with the UK and the US falling a long way behind. Surprisingly, the Italian workers seem to have benefited most in this period, having quadrupled their real wages. Similarly, the West German, French and Japanese had large increases, while the US workers suffered a smaller increase than even the UK.

Data

Increase in real earnings, calculated by dividing the wage rate index by the retail price index, for the years 1966 and 1975.

Source

UN Statistical Yearbook

Real wage increases since 1953

1966

France
West Germany
Italy
Japan
UK
US

1975

France
West Germany
Italy
Japan
UK
US

Real earnings		1966	1975
All based on 1953 = 100	France	161	269
	West Germany	209	311
	Italy	158	439
	Japan	166	315
	UK	151	207
	US	130	139

The previous topic (75) is useful for showing the differential rates of growth in real earnings in different countries. However, it cannot tell us anything about the *absolute* levels of real earning power.

Here we use the same technique as that employed in topic 70: it shows how long it takes to earn sufficient money to buy certain basic foodstuffs in different countries. Here again, two alternative presentations are given: the unbracketed figures ignore the effects of tax—that is, they relate to *gross* earnings; the bracketed figures incorporate the effects of tax—that is, they relate to *net* earnings.

The gross earnings figures show that tea is 'cheapest' in the UK, while the UK also fares particularly well (relative to the other European countries and to Japan) with respect to cheese, beef and bread.

The position changes somewhat when the effects of taxation are taken into account. According to figures published by the OECD, the average production worker in the UK gives up some 23 per cent of his gross earnings in the form of income tax and national insurance contributions; the corresponding figures for the other countries portrayed are: Canada, 16 per cent; France, 8 per cent; West Germany, 23 per cent; Italy, 12 per cent; Japan, 9 per cent; and the US, 17 per cent. When these deductions are taken into account, the UK loses its position as cheapest in tea to Italy, and generally becomes more expensive relative to all countries except West Germany. Nevertheless, the UK is still relatively cheap for some items—beef is an obvious example.

Data

The price data relate to October 1977. The earnings data is, whenever possible, the average earnings of persons (males and females averaged) in non-agricultural sectors. The earnings data is mainly for October 1977. The tax figures assume a married man with two children; the tax data relate to 1974.

Where possible, standardized commodities are used. However, this is not always possible: as is well-known, a French loaf is rather different from an English loaf! Finally, it should be noted that inferences can *not* be made from this information about the time-cost of goods not portrayed here; as in any study where particular examples are chosen the results *may* be unrepresentative. (For example, while beef may be relatively expensive in France and West Germany, it *may* be the case that cars, say, are relatively cheap; however, it is very difficult to make this latter comparison because a French or German car is not the same as a British one.)

Sources

Bulletin of Labour Statistics
OECD *Revenue Statistics* 1965–74

Milk (litre)		
Canada	5.8 mins	(6.9)
France	8.8 mins	(9.6)
West Germany	5.4 mins	(7.0)
Italy	7.8 mins	(8.9)
Japan	16.3 mins	(17.9)
UK	8.3 mins	(10.8)
US	5.0 mins	(6.0)

Bread (kilogram white)		
Canada	6.4 mins	(7.6)
France	18.5 mins	(20.1)
West Germany	15.0 mins	(19.5)
Italy	12.4 mins	(14.1)
Japan	17.6 mins	(19.3)
UK	12.0 mins	(15.6)
US	8.7 mins	(10.5)

Cheese (kilogram)		
Canada	35.3 mins	(42.0)
France	102.2 mins	(111.1)
West Germany	69.9 mins	(90.8)
Italy	159.4 mins	(181.1)
Japan	71.5 mins	(78.6)
UK	69.9 mins	(79.1)
US	42.8 mins	(51.6)

Beef (kilogram sirloin)		
Canada	49.7 mins	(59.1)
France	168.9 mins	(183.6)
West Germany	157.8 mins	(205.0)
Italy	115.8 mins	(131.5)
Japan	331.0 mins	(363.8)
UK	128.2 mins	(166.5)
US	46.9 mins	(56.5)

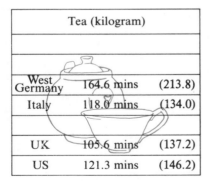

Tea (kilogram)		
West Germany	164.6 mins	(213.8)
Italy	118.0 mins	(134.0)
UK	105.6 mins	(137.2)
US	121.3 mins	(146.2)

Eggs (kilogram)		
Canada	4.1 mins	(4.9)
France	2.8 mins	(3.0)
West Germany	7.9 mins	(10.3)
Italy	1.8 mins	(2.0)
Japan	8.5 mins	(9.3)
UK	9.4 mins	(12.2)
US	4.0 mins	(4.8)

Having looked at international trends in earnings rates and retail prices, it is now useful to look at the trend in UK average weekly earnings since 1948, and then, by deflating these by the retail price index, obtain a real average earnings pattern. First, the figures for average weekly earnings of male manual workers were obtained and plotted on a simple graph, with average earnings on the vertical axis and years on the horizontal.

From this graph it can be seen that average earnings in money terms (that is, without adjustment being made for inflation) were rising at a steady, if relatively slow, rate for some years until 1969 and 1970, when a sharp rise in the rate of increase in money wages occurred, which continued to 1977. This period corresponded to the boom of the early 1970s, which was accompanied by a sharp rise in the rate of inflation. This is shown when the trend of real average earnings is examined. As can be seen, there is an upward trend in the real average earnings, although it is a slow and steady one. Again, in 1970 and thereafter, a slight rise in the rate of increase of real earnings occurs, reaching a peak in 1974. However, for each of two subsequent years the real average earnings fell, reflecting the high rate of inflation that began to outstrip wage increases. The effect of this is to bring the value of average weekly earnings, in real terms, for 1977 down to the equivalent mid-1971 rate.

Data

Average weekly earnings of full-time manual workers in all industries covered by Department of Employment surveys, also deflated by the retail price index.

Source

Department of Employment Gazette, May 1978

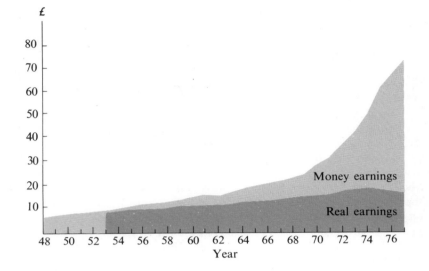

Year	48	49	50	51	52	53	54	55	56	57
Average weekly earnings £	6.90	7.13	7.52	8.30	8.93	9.46	10.22	11.15	11.90	12.58
Real weekly earnings						9.46	10.12	10.51	10.63	10.94

Year	58	59	60	61	62	63	64	65	66	67
Average weekly earnings	12.83	13.54	14.53	15.34	15.86	16.75	18.11	19.59	20.30	21.38
Real weekly earnings	10.78	11.28	12.00	12.27	12.20	12.59	13.21	13.60	13.62	13.97

Year	68	69	70	71	72	73	74	75	76	77
Average weekly earnings	23.00	24.82	28.05	30.93	35.82	40.92	48.63	59.58	66.97	72.89
Real weekly earnings	14.38	14.69	15.58	15.78	17.06	17.79	18.28	18.05	17.27	16.23

The purpose of this section is to show how family expenditure on various groups of consumer items has changed over a period of time when real incomes have been steadily rising. This pattern is presented as the percentage of total consumer expenditure that households in the survey spent on seven major expenditure groups:

(i) food
(ii) clothing and footwear
(iii) housing
(iv) alcohol and tobacco
(v) fuel and light
(vi) household durables
(vii) other expenditure, including entertainment, travel, etc.

A cross-section analysis of the average family's expenditure pattern is obtained from the Family Expenditure Survey, and this is presented for the years 1951 and 1976 in the form of a pie chart. Each slice of the pie has an area that corresponds to the percentage of expenditure on a particular group. The pie for 1976 is larger because the total consumer's expenditure increased in real terms between 1951 and 1976.

From the charts it can be seen that the proportion spent on food and clothing has declined, as is to be expected during a period of rising incomes. More surprisingly, percentage expenditure on tobacco and alcohol is also less, representing a rise in abstemiousness, perhaps? The increase in percentages spent on fuel and light may possibly reflect an increase in the use of electrical gadgets and central heating, whilst the increase in expenditure on housing may be due to an increasing tendency towards home ownership.

Data

Consumer's expenditure (as a percentage of the total) for 1951 and 1976. Because of the effects of the war (rationing and release of constrained purchasing power) 1951 figures may be slightly distorted.

Source

Social Trends, 1970, 1977

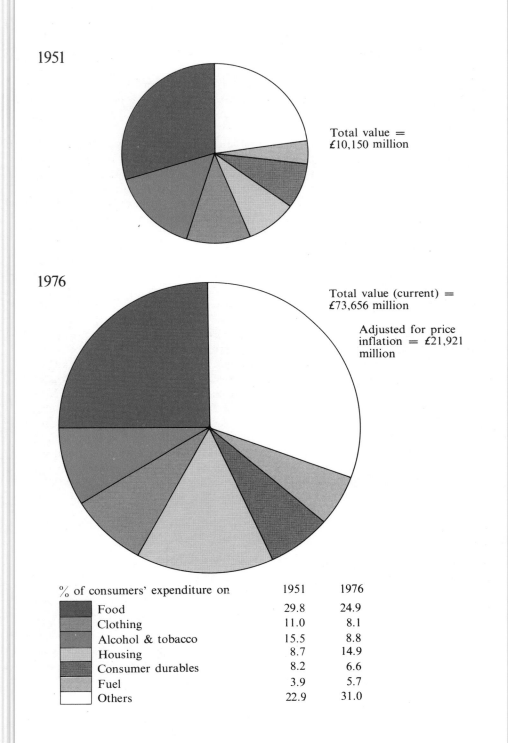

1951

Total value =
£10,150 million

1976

Total value (current) =
£73,656 million

Adjusted for price
inflation = £21,921
million

% of consumers' expenditure on	1951	1976
Food	29.8	24.9
Clothing	11.0	8.1
Alcohol & tobacco	15.5	8.8
Housing	8.7	14.9
Consumer durables	8.2	6.6
Fuel	3.9	5.7
Others	22.9	31.0

There are differences in the legal and judicial systems of England and Wales, Scotland and Northern Ireland that make it impossible to provide data for the UK as a whole. These differences concern the classification of offences and the meanings of certain terms.

The pie charts on the left-hand side of the page give persons found guilty of offences per 1,000 population, split by age and sex for 1976. The size of the pie charts for males and females is proportional to the number of indictable offences in England and Wales, and to the number of crimes in Scotland. The vast majority of offences are committed by young men and boys. The age groups collected for England and Wales and for Scotland are different because of differences in the ways child offenders are treated. The Social Work (Scotland) Act 1968 introduced a system of children's hearings, and children under 16 no longer appear before a court unless the charge is a particularly serious one.

The other pie charts give the types of offence as known to the police in 1976. Both for Scotland, and for England and Wales, it is the various types of theft that form the majority of offences (see *Data* section). The percentage of indictable offences cleared up in England and Wales was 43 per cent in 1976. The proportion has been fairly stable for over 20 years—in 1951 it was 47 per cent, fell to 39 per cent in 1966 and has risen again since. Scotland does not fare so well. In 1976 only 31.5 per cent of their crimes were cleared up and it has been falling steadily since 1951.

The graph gives the number of persons found guilty of violence against the person—this includes murder, manslaughter and wounding. The data runs from 1938 and 1948 through to 1976. The increase in violent crimes has continued steadily over the years apart from an exceptional increase in 1973. Most of this is due to an increase in the number found guilty of wounding, though there is no evident explanation for this. (The reader might like to try to infer from this graph the date of the abolition of the death penalty!)

Data

'Non-indictable offences' in England and Wales, and 'Miscellaneous offences' in Scotland are *excluded* from this analysis; these categories cover a multitude of sins, including motoring offences, drunkenness, and so on.

The comparison of criminal statistics for England and Wales and for Scotland is hazardous, but was carried out in the *Annual Abstract of Statistics* until 1969. Any comparison of statistics taken before with those taken after that date would be rendered almost meaningless by the re-definition of theft in the Theft Act of January 1969.

Sources

Annual Abstract of Statistics
Social Trends

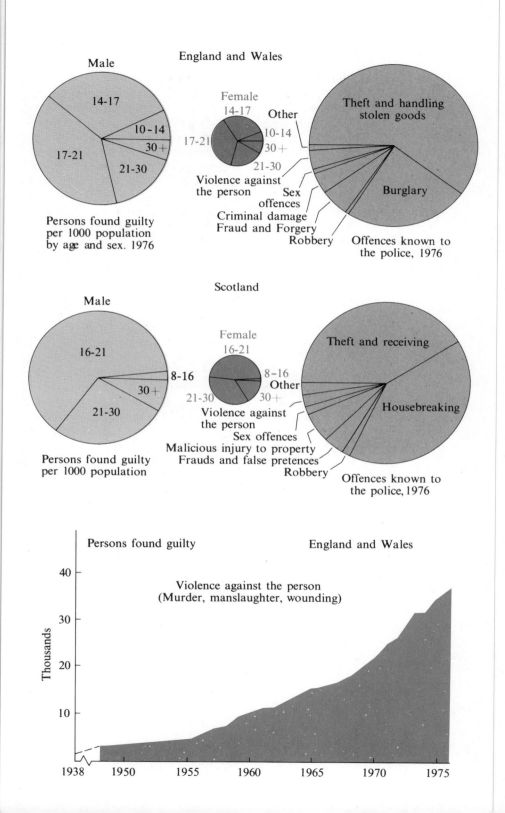

Male

England and Wales

14-17

10 - 14

30+

17-21

21-30

Persons found guilty
per 1000 population
by age and sex. 1976

Female
14-17   Other
                 10-14
17-21   30+
                 21-30
Violence against
the person   Sex
                  offences
     Criminal damage
  Fraud and Forgery
          Robbery

Theft and handling
stolen goods

Burglary

Offences known to
the police, 1976

Scotland

Male

16-21

8-16

30+

21-30

Persons found guilty
per 1000 population

Female
16-21
                 8–16
                 Other
21-30   30+
Violence against
the person
          Sex offences
Malicious injury to property
   Frauds and false pretences
          Robbery

Theft and receiving

Housebreaking

Offences known to
the police, 1976

Persons found guilty   England and Wales

40

Violence against the person
(Murder, manslaughter, wounding)

30

Thousands

20

10

1938   1950   1955   1960   1965   1970   1975

The data used is for passenger vehicles only; it does not include goods vehicles as this and the next two topics are concerned with international comparisons of the various forms of passenger transport. There are many factors that influence the choice of transport within a country: its population size, its surface area and its national income, to name a few. The US has always led in the personal use of cars. The diagram opposite shows the number of cars per head of population for various countries. The increase in the number of cars per head was very rapid in all countries over the period 1959 to 1974. It must be pointed out that India is on a different scale (the right-hand axis) to that of the others. Its very large population and position of poverty relative to the developed countries means that if it were plotted on the same scale it would lie along the horizontal axis. So, although its growth has been rapid, it is still far behind the other countries. The UK has had a steady growth in number of cars per head, but Germany and Italy increased their totals at a faster rate, to overtake the UK—Germany in 1968 and Italy in 1972.

The absolute difference between the countries can be seen more clearly in the bar chart. The US had 104 million cars on its roads in 1974 compared to 700,000 in India. In order for this enormous number of cars to be used there have been massive road-building schemes all over the US. Most major US cities have large freeways systems. Dallas and Los Angeles are extreme examples: 50 per cent of their land space is covered by road networks! Japan has a large number of cars but because of its large population appears at the bottom of the cars per head diagram. Pollution from car exhausts is a major problem in many cities. Los Angeles and Tokyo (where in 1971 many people started wearing gas-masks) are both famous for their smogs.

Data

The major problem, that India is so much below the other nations, has been mentioned above. The use of two vertical scales, the right-hand one for India and the left-hand for the others, should be noted.

The 1973 and 1974 values for India are just estimates. The fall from 1972 to 1973 is, in fact, a small one but is exaggerated by the scaling difference.

Source

UN Statistical Yearbook

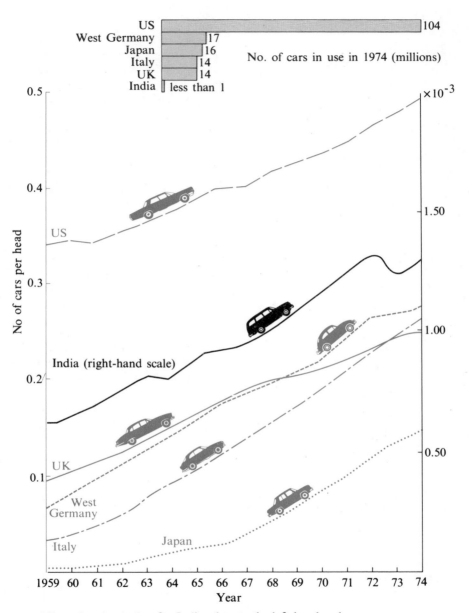

No. of cars in use in 1974 (millions)

US	104
West Germany	17
Japan	16
Italy	14
UK	14
India	less than 1

US

India (right-hand scale)

UK

West Germany

Italy

Japan

No of cars per head

0.5 — 0.4 — 0.3 — 0.2 — 0.1 —

×10⁻³ — 1.50 — 1.00 — 0.50

1959 60 61 62 63 64 65 66 67 68 69 70 71 72 73 74

Year

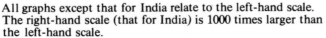

All graphs except that for India relate to the left-hand scale.
The right-hand scale (that for India) is 1000 times larger than
the left-hand scale.

In this section it is again necessary to use two different scales. The US dominates this form of passenger transport by air completely, as can be seen from the bar chart. The scale on the right, which is used to plot the US values, is therefore ten times greater than the scale on the left. Both scales are measured in millions of passenger kilometres per year. All countries have increased their air travel rapidly since 1959. The UK was far ahead of the other countries, except for the US, in 1959 but since then the gap has lessened. Japan, in particular, has expanded its air transport very quickly since 1966 and has now overtaken the UK. India has the lowest level of service but the difference between the countries is not as marked as with car transport.

Data

The figures give total scheduled services for civil aviation. This includes international and home flights. If only international flights were used then the US would not be so far ahead of the others, as the majority of US flights are internal. For example, in 1974, the US flights totalled 262 million passenger-kilometres, but only 45 million of these were international. The UK carried out 27 million passenger-kilometres in the same year, 25 million of which were international. This marks the greatest difference between US travel and travel in the other countries. Because of the large surface area of the US, internal travel is commonplace, whereas in the other countries it is still rare.

Source

UN Statistical Yearbook

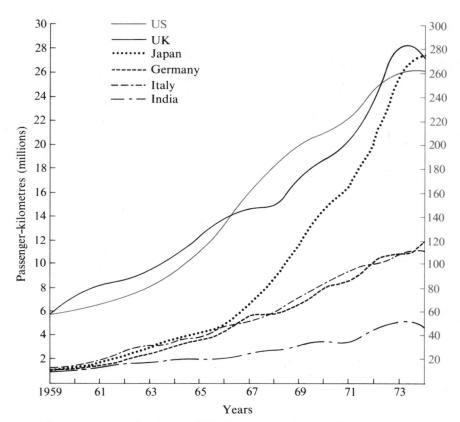

All graphs except that for the US relate to the left-hand scale.
The right-hand scale (that for the US) is 10 times larger than
the left-hand scale.

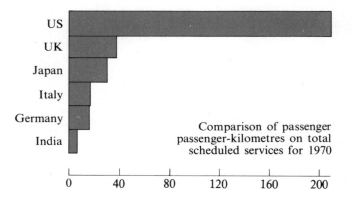

Comparison of passenger
passenger-kilometres on total
scheduled services for 1970

In the developed countries, rail is usually thought of as a declining form of passenger transport. From the diagram, it can be seen that Germany, Italy and the UK have had very little change in the number of railway passenger-kilometres per year. As travel has, in general, been increasing, this does show a relative decline. These three countries are similar in terms of population size and surface area, as seen from the bar chart above. It is too early to see if the use of high-speed trains in the UK will affect the use of rail transport for passengers.

The US has been declining steadily in its use of rail as a means of personal transport. It is a very large country with a relatively small population: its population density is only 23 people per square kilometre, while the population density of the UK is 229 people per square kilometre. Air travel is by far the most convenient for high density conurbations with vast empty expanses between them. The US also has a sophisticated network of inter-state highways so that long distance car-travel is relatively easy.

Japan is far and away the leading exponent of rail transport. It has the high population density of around 300 people per square kilometre. A third of its 109 million population live in the Tokaido conurbation, which includes Tokyo, Yokohama and Osaka. Many of these commute to the centre and of these, 75 per cent commute by rail.

As India is a poor country, there is relatively little travel. Internal travel is done mostly by rail and so passenger-kilometres per year is high with respect to the totals for other developed countries.

Data

The figures are given in millions of passenger-kilometres per year, so they are comparable with those of air transport.

Source

UN Statistical Yearbook

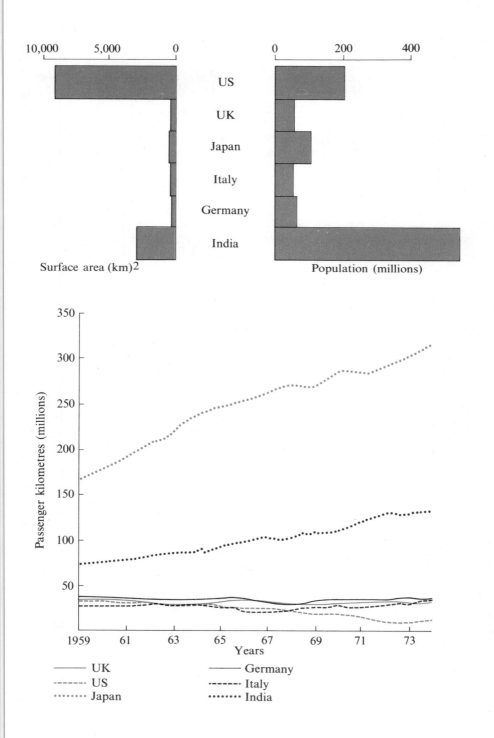

From the table opposite, it can be seen that in the 10 years 1964–74, the number killed, seriously injured and slightly injured in road accidents in the UK have all fallen slightly despite the rise in the number of cars on the road. The numbers involved are very large compared to the numbers killed and injured by other forms of transport. For example, in 1974 the number of deaths due to train accidents was 6, and 4 of these were railway servants. There were, however, 283 deaths of trespassers or suicides. Similarly, accidents on scheduled passenger-carrying services are negligible.

Approximately half of all fatal injuries due to road accidents involve persons under the age of 20. The numbers of very young children is relatively low as they are usually accompanied by an adult. The large number of 16- and 17–19-year-olds killed is mostly due to deaths of young motor-cyclists and car drivers and passengers. The proportion of young people who are seriously injured is even higher, around two-thirds of the total in 1976.

When the data is split by type of road user, it is car and taxi drivers and passengers that make up the largest proportion of fatal and seriously injured persons. This has been rising sharply over the years. In 1968, legislation was introduced to make the fitting of seat-belts compulsory. A survey carried out in April 1974 showed that 27 per cent of drivers wore belts on all journeys; 39 per cent did on all motorway journeys. Pedestrian deaths have been falling slowly. The increasing use of pelican crossings, the advertised 'Green Cross Code', may be having an effect.

It looks at first sight as though the number of motor-cycle accidents is small but when the number of motor-cycles on the road is compared to the number of cars, then the proportion of motor-cyclists involved in accidents is high. In 1970 there were over 12 million cars and just over 1 million motor-cycles.

Data

Persons who die more than one month after the accident are included in the figures for the injured and not for deaths.

It may be of interest to note that during the period 1964 to 1974 the annual number killed in road accidents fluctuated (fairly randomly) between 6,810 and 7,985, while the number seriously injured fluctuated between 88,563 and 99,838. Time series graphs of these two variables reveal no obvious effect of the breathalyzer and of varying speed limits. (This is not to deny that they may have had an effect; but, if so, it was swamped by other factors.)

Sources

Annual Abstract of Statistics
Social Trends

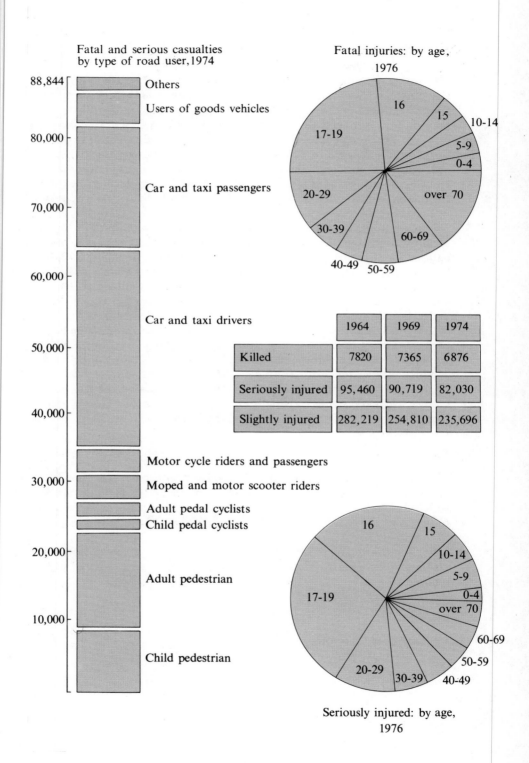

Fatal and serious casualties by type of road user, 1974

88,844 — Others

Users of goods vehicles

80,000 —

Car and taxi passengers

70,000 —

60,000 —

Car and taxi drivers

50,000 —

40,000 —

Motor cycle riders and passengers

30,000 — Moped and motor scooter riders

Adult pedal cyclists

Child pedal cyclists

20,000 —

Adult pedestrian

10,000 —

Child pedestrian

Fatal injuries: by age, 1976

16, 15, 10-14, 5-9, 0-4, over 70, 60-69, 50-59, 40-49, 30-39, 20-29, 17-19

	1964	1969	1974
Killed	7820	7365	6876
Seriously injured	95,460	90,719	82,030
Slightly injured	282,219	254,810	235,696

Seriously injured: by age, 1976

16, 15, 10-14, 5-9, 0-4, over 70, 60-69, 50-59, 40-49, 30-39, 20-29, 17-19

The time series opposite gives the total number of tourists who visited the UK between 1948 and 1975. These are people who are permanently resident abroad and who visit the UK for less than 12 months, for a holiday, for business trips, for study, etc. In 1948, the UK was visited by only half a million people. This number has risen rapidly ever since due to world-wide increases in travel generally. In recent years this has been encouraged by greater links with European countries through the EEC and EFTA and also because the exchange rate between sterling and other European and North American currencies made holidays for foreigners in Britain relatively cheap.

Foreign tourists are a major source of foreign currency. In 1974 tourist receipts for the UK were almost $2 billion. The bar chart gives data of the nationalities of tourists to the UK for 1975 and 1964. In 1975, 1,350,000 US tourists visited the UK compared to only 590,000 in 1964. The number of German and French visitors has increased even faster. The six countries shown account for almost 5 million visitors out of a total of under 9 million for 1975.

The final bar chart gives the countries to which Britons travel in order of popularity. Spain is by far the most popular holiday resort for Britons; it includes the Spanish mainland and the Balearic Isles, Majorca and Minorca. France receives visits from $1\frac{1}{2}$ million Britons and Belgium from $1\frac{1}{4}$ million. The figures given are for 1975. The number of visitors to Greece has been increasing rapidly as it has only in recent years become a tourist centre. About 60,000 Britons visited the USSR in 1975.

Data

The United Nations Statistical Yearbook lists two broad ways of counting the number of visits to a country. One is by means of frontier checks, which should be fairly accurate; the other is hotel records, which will be rather inaccurate as many people travel to stay with relatives or to go camping, etc.

For visitors to the UK, frontier checks are used, but numbers of Britons visiting other countries are sometimes calculated using various hotel records.

Sources

UN Statistical Yearbooks

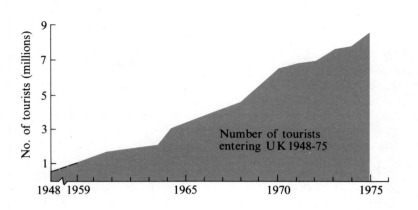

No. of tourists (millions)

Number of tourists
entering UK 1948-75

1948 1959   1965   1970   1975

Visitors to UK by country of origin

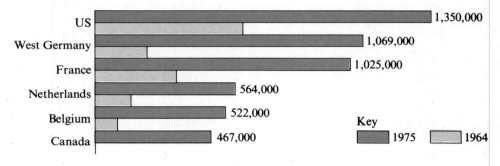

US — 1,350,000
West Germany — 1,069,000
France — 1,025,000
Netherlands — 564,000
Belgium — 522,000
Canada — 467,000

Key   ▓ 1975   ░ 1964

British visitors to other countries, 1975

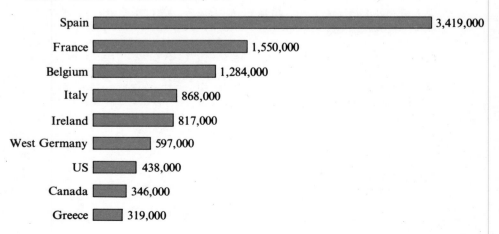

Spain — 3,419,000
France — 1,550,000
Belgium — 1,284,000
Italy — 868,000
Ireland — 817,000
West Germany — 597,000
US — 438,000
Canada — 346,000
Greece — 319,000

The bar chart gives the number of daily newspapers per 1,000 inhabitants in several countries for the years 1960 or 1961 and 1972 or 1973. There seems to be no overall world-wide pattern of change. For some countries, including the UK and the US, the number of newspapers has fallen. This may be because increased numbers of persons have access to other media, particularly the television. Japan, on the other hand, now has more than one newspaper for every two inhabitants. Italy has a surprisingly low circulation of newspapers.

The pie charts give a breakdown of sales of daily and Sunday newspapers in the UK. It is useful to split the data into 'quality' press and 'mass circulation' newspapers. The 'quality' press have a smaller proportion of total sales than do the mass circulation newspapers. Newspaper reading depends to a large extent on social class. In general, the higher your social class the more likely you are to read any daily newspaper, and also the more likely you are to read a 'quality' newspaper. For example, the percentage of the whole population reading the *Daily Telegraph* is on average only 8 per cent, whereas 33 per cent of the highest class read it and only 2 per cent of the lowest class do. (See *Data* section.) 30 per cent of the population read the *Sun*, but only 5 per cent of the highest class do. People are more likely to read a Sunday newspaper than a daily newspaper irrespective of class. The class distinction is still there, however, with 45 per cent of the top class reading the *Sunday Times* compared with 2 per cent of the lowest class.

Data

The international data is given for 1960 in some countries and 1961 in others. There is a similar problem for the 1970s data.

The social gradings used in the National Readership Survey is: Class A (the 'highest' category discussed above) the head of the household is a successful businessman, or professional man, senior civil servant or has considerable private means; covers about 3 per cent of the population.

Class E (the 'lowest' discussed above) old-age pensioners, widows, casual workers and those on social security with household income little above basic flat rate social security benefit; covers about 9 per cent of the population.

Sources

Social Trends
UN Statistical Yearbook

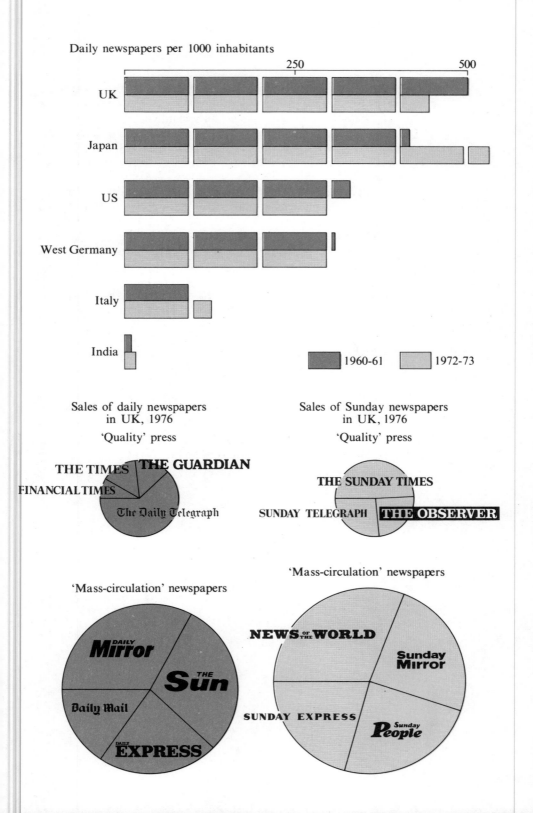

Daily newspapers per 1000 inhabitants

250　　　　　　　　500

UK

Japan

US

West Germany

Italy

India

■ 1960-61　　□ 1972-73

Sales of daily newspapers
in UK, 1976

'Quality' press

THE TIMES　THE GUARDIAN
FINANCIAL TIMES
The Daily Telegraph

Sales of Sunday newspapers
in UK, 1976

'Quality' press

THE SUNDAY TIMES
SUNDAY TELEGRAPH　THE OBSERVER

'Mass-circulation' newspapers

DAILY Mirror
THE Sun
Daily Mail
DAILY EXPRESS

'Mass-circulation' newspapers

NEWS of the WORLD
Sunday Mirror
SUNDAY EXPRESS
Sunday People

The number of cinemas and per capita attendance in cinemas has been declining in most of the Western world since the mid-1950s, when television sets became easily attainable. Of the countries shown it is only India whose attendance has risen, but this is mostly due to the fact that there are still very few televisions available in India. The US is the only country to have large numbers of drive-in movies, although the numbers of these are declining.

In the UK the decline in admissions has been accompanied by an increase in the number of television licence holders. In 1960, 10½ million television licenses were issued. By 1977, the number was over 18 million and in July 1976, the number of licences for colour exceeded that for black and white for the first time. In a study in February 1977, it was found that for the population aged 5 and over, on average 20 hours a week was spent watching television.

The majority of people going to the cinema are between the ages of 16 and 25. Very few older people go to the cinema. The regional analysis of admissions to cinemas in the UK for 1975 shows that a very large proportion occur in the south-east, including Greater London, even though the average price of admission was higher there than anywhere else at 80.28p in 1975. Wales, on the other hand, has a low number of admissions but the price is low at 45.45p on average.

Data

The data for India includes a large number of mobile cinemas. The data for the US excludes the drive-in cinemas.

Sources

UN Statistical Yearbook
Social Trends
Regional Statistics

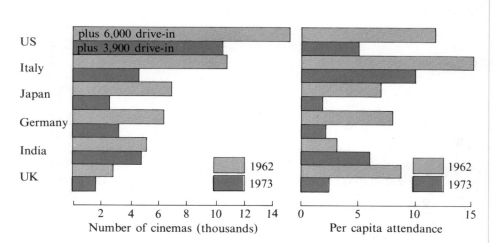

Number of cinemas (thousands) Per capita attendance

US
Italy
Japan
Germany
India
UK

plus 6,000 drive-in
plus 3,900 drive-in

1962
1973

Table: Percentage population going to the cinema:
by age and sex

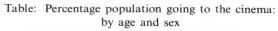

Percentage going to cinema by age:	Male	Female
16-19	31	38
20-24	26	25
25-29	18	15
30-44	10	12
45-59	6	5
60-69	3	3
70+	1	1

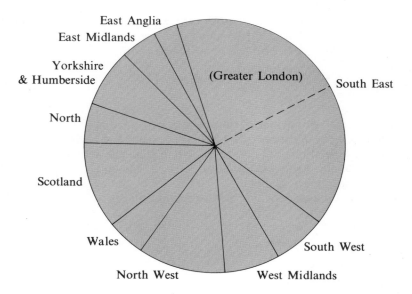

Regional analysis of admissions to cinemas in UK, 1975

The two time trend graphs give the percentage of pupils remaining at school beyond the statutory leaving age for (a) maintained schools and (b) non-maintained schools for the years 1965 and 1970 to 1976. (The leaving age changed from 15 to 16 in 1974, as shown in diagram.) More pupils stay on in the private sector schools at all ages. The general trend is a slow rise over time in the number staying at school, apart from a marked decrease for 16-year-olds in 1974—this is just a result of changing the leaving age.

The split pie charts give the destinations on leaving school in 1975–76 by type of school and sex. It must be stressed that the numbers of pupils in the types of schools are different:

490,000 pupils in Comprehensive
107,000 pupils in Modern
48,000 pupils in Grammar
27,500 pupils in Direct Grant
15,700 pupils in Independent Schools

N.B. No 'Modern' pie chart is given, as very few pupils do anything other than go straight into employment. Only 0.2 per cent go on to degree courses; 0.1 per cent go into teaching; 14 per cent go into other further education.

A greater percentage of boys go on to degree courses than girls do, whatever the type of school they attend. Direct Grant schools have the highest percentage with 45.2 per cent of the boys and 33 per cent of the girls. Grammar schools have 31 per cent of the boys and 19 per cent of the girls going on to degree courses. Comprehensive schools have only 5.8 per cent of the boys and 3.6 per cent of the girls. This is misleading, however, because the Grammar school children are screened before admission. There are no figures for the percentage of children in the top streams of comprehensives going to degree courses.

More girls than boys go on to teacher training whatever the type of school.

Data

The term 'employment' includes temporary employment pending entry to full-time education, other destinations and destinations unknown. The figures given may, therefore, be larger than the actual ones.

Maintained schools include Grammar, Modern, Comprehensive and other secondary schools.

Only Independent Schools that are recognized as efficient are included in the statistics.

Source

Statistics of Education

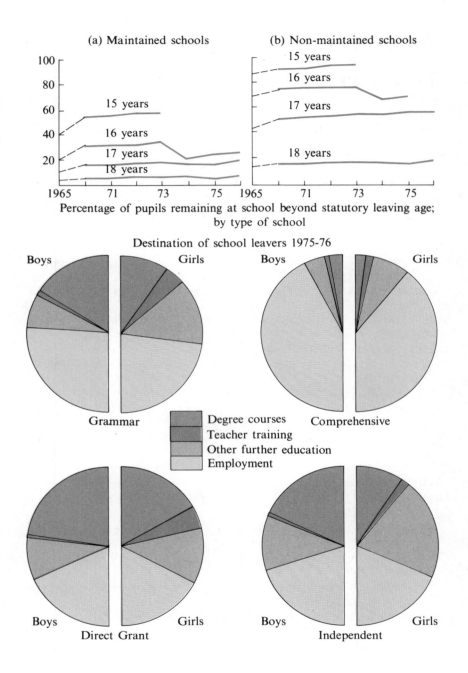

(a) Maintained schools   (b) Non-maintained schools

Percentage of pupils remaining at school beyond statutory leaving age;
by type of school

Destination of school leavers 1975-76

Grammar

Comprehensive

Degree courses
Teacher training
Other further education
Employment

Direct Grant

Independent

BIBLIOGRAPHY

This bibliography is in two parts. The first part contains the sources of virtually all the information presented in the book; all these items are official publications that appear on a regular (usually annually or quarterly) basis. The second part contains references to other (usually very minor) source material, and some general references which may be of interest.

1. Official statistical periodical publications

Bank of England, *Bank of England Quarterly Bulletin*, Bank of England, London, 1961–.

Bank of England, *Statistical Abstract*, Bank of England, London, 1970, 1974.

Board of Trade, *Statistical Abstract for the United Kingdom*, HMSO, London, 1840–1938.

Central Statistical Office, *Abstract of Regional Statistics*, HMSO, London, 1965–1974.

Central Statistical Office, *Annual Abstract of Statistics*, HMSO, London, 1935–.

Central Statistical Office, *Economic Trends*, HMSO, London, 1958–.

Central Statistical Office, *Economic Trends Annual Supplement*, HMSO, London, 1975–.

Central Statistical Office, *Financial Statistics*, HMSO, London, 1962–.

Central Statistical Office, *Monthly Digest of Statistics*, HMSO, London, 1948–.

Central Statistical Office, *National Income and Expenditure*, HMSO, London, 1946–.

Central Statistical Office, *Regional Statistics*, HMSO, London, 1975–.

Central Statistical Office, *Social Trends, HMSO,* London, 1970–.

Central Statistical Office, *United Kingdom Balance of Payments*, HMSO, London, 1963–.

Department of Education and Science, *Statistics of Education*, HMSO, London, 1961–.

Department of Employment, *British Labour Statistics Yearbook*, HMSO, London, 1969–.

Department of Employment, *Department of Employment Gazette*, HMSO, London, 1971–.

Department of Employment, *Family Expenditure Survey*, HMSO, London, 1957/9–.

Department of Employment, *New Earnings Survey*, HMSO, London, 1968–.

Department of Employment and Productivity, *British Labour Statistics Historical Abstract 1886–1968*, HMSO, London, 1971.

International Labour Organization, *Bulletin of Labour Statistics*, ILO, Geneva, 1972–.

International Labour Organization, *Year Book of Labour Statistics*, ILO, Geneva, 1936–.

Ministry of Agriculture, Fisheries and Food, *Household Food Consumption and Expenditure*, HMSO, London, 1940–.

Office of Population Censuses and Surveys, *General Household Survey*, HMSO, London, 1975–.

Office of Population Censuses and Surveys, *OPCS Monitor*, HMSO, London, 1975–.

Office of Population Censuses and Surveys, *Population Trends*, HMSO, London, 1975–.

Office of Population Censuses and Surveys, *Registrar General's Decennial Supplement, England and Wales*, HMSO, London, 1961–.

Office of Population Censuses and Surveys, *Registrar General's Statistical Review of England and Wales*, HMSO, London, 1968–.

Office of Population Censuses and Surveys, *Trends in Mortality*, 1951–1975, Series DHI, no. 3, HMSO, London.

Registrar General of England and Wales, *Annual Report*, HMSO, London, 1839–.

United Nations Statistical Office, *Demographic Yearbook*, UN, New York, 1948–.

United Nations Statistical Office, *Monthly Bulletin of Statistics*, UN, New York, 1947–.

United Nations Statistical Office, *Statistical Yearbook*, UN, New York, 1949–.

United Nations Statistical Office, *Yearbook of International Trade Statistics*, UN, New York, 1950–.

United Nations Statistical Office, *Yearbook of National Accounts Statistics*, UN, New York, 1961–.

World Health Organization, *Suicide and Attempted Suicide*, Public Health paper no. 58, WHO, Geneva, 1974.

2. *Other reference material and supplementary bibliography*

Alderson, M., *An Introduction to Epidemiology*, Macmillan, London, 1976.

Atkinson, A. B. and Harrison, A. J., *Distribution of Personal Wealth in Britain*, Cambridge U.P., 1978.

Bannock, G., Baxter, R. E., and Rees, R., *The Penguin Dictionary of Economics*, Penguin, Harmondsworth, 1972.

Barker, D. J. P. and Rose, G., *Epidemiology in Medical Practice*, Churchill Livingstone, London, 1976.

Butler, D. and Freeman, J., *British Political Facts 1900–1968*, Macmillan, London, 1968.

Central Office of Information, *Britain: An Official Handbook*, HMSO, London, 1964–.

Central Statistical Office, *Guide to Official Statistics*, HMSO, London, 1976.

Donaldson, P., *Guide to the British Economy*, 3rd ed., Penguin, Harmondsworth, 1971.

Europa, *The Europa Year Book*, Europa, London, 1962–.

Fischer, R. L., *Defending the Central Front: The Balance of Forces*, Adelphi Paper no. 127, International Institute for Strategic Studies, 1976.

Houses of Commons and Lords, *Hansard*, HMSO, London.

London and Cambridge Economic Service, *The British Economy Key Statistics 1900–1970*, Times Newspapers, London.

Maunder, W. F. (ed.), *Reviews of United Kingdom Statistical Sources*, vols. 1–5, Heinemann, London, 1974–76.

Morris, D. (ed.), *The Economic System in the United Kingdom*, Oxford U.P., Oxford, 1977.

Nutter, G. Warren, *Growth of Government in the West*, American Enterprise Institute for Public Policy Research, AEI studies no. 185, 1978.

Organization for Economic and Cultural Development, *Revenue Statistics*, OECD, Paris, 1972–.

Ward, B., *The Home of Man*, Penguin, Harmondsworth, 1976.

INDEX

Note: references given are to TOPIC NUMBERS

186